HOW TO
KEEP
CALM
AND
CARRY
ON

PEARSON

At Pearson, we believe in learning – all kinds of learning for all kinds of people. Whether it's at home, in the classroom or in the workplace, learning is the key to improving our life chances.

That's why we're working with leading authors to bring you the latest thinking and the best practices, so you can get better at the things that are important to you. You can learn on the page or on the move, and with content that's always crafted to help you understand quickly and apply what you've learned.

If you want to upgrade your personal skills or accelerate your career, become a more effective leader or more powerful communicator, discover new opportunities or simply find more inspiration, we can help you make progress in your work and life.

Pearson is the world's leading learning company. Our portfolio includes the Financial Times, Penguin, Dorling Kindersley, and our educational business, Pearson International.

Every day our work helps learning flourish, and wherever learning flourishes, so do people.

To learn more please visit us at: **www.pearson.com/uk**

HOW TO
KEEP
CALM
AND
CARRY
ON

Inspiring ways to worry less and live a happier life

PROFESSOR DANIEL FREEMAN
JASON FREEMAN

PEARSON

Harlow, England • London • New York • Boston • San Francisco • Toronto • Sydney
Auckland • Singapore • Hong Kong • Tokyo • Seoul • Taipei • New Delhi
Cape Town • São Paulo • Mexico City • Madrid • Amsterdam • Munich • Paris • Milan

PEARSON EDUCATION LIMITED

Edinburgh Gate
Harlow CM20 2JE
United Kingdom
Tel: +44 (0)1279 623623
Web: www.pearson.com/uk

First published 2013 (print and electronic)

ISBN: 978-0-273-77775-5 (print)
      978-0-273-77853-0 (PDF)
      978-0-273-77852-3 (ePub)
      978-1-292-00731-1 (eText)

British Library Cataloguing-in-Publication Data
A catalogue record for the print edition is available from the British Library

Library of Congress Cataloging-in-Publication Data
Freeman, Jason (Jason Ryan)
  How to keep calm and carry on : inspiring ways to worry less and live a happier life / Jason Freeman, Professor Daniel Freeman.
     pages cm
  ISBN 978-0-273-77775-5
  1. Anxiety. 2. Worry. 3. Stress management. I. Freeman, Daniel, 1971- II. Title.
  BF575.A6F735 2013
  152.4'6--dc23

                   2013014483

10 9 8 7 6 5 4 3 2 1
17 16 15 14 13

Text design by Design Deluxe
Cover design by Two Associates
Cover image © iStockPhoto.com/Adriana Berned

Print edition typeset in Gill Sans MT Std 11/14pt by 3
Print edition printed and bound in Great Britain by Clays Ltd., Bungay, Suffolk.

NOTE THAT ANY PAGE CROSS REFERENCES REFER TO THE PRINT EDITION

CONTENTS

ABOUT THE
AUTHORS

Daniel Freeman is a Professor of Clinical Psychology and a Medical Research Council (MRC) Senior Clinical Fellow in the Department of Psychiatry at the University of Oxford, and a Fellow of University College, Oxford. He is also an honorary consultant clinical psychologist in Oxford Health NHS Foundation Trust.

Jason Freeman is a writer and editor in the areas of popular psychology and self-help.

Daniel and Jason are the authors of:

★ *The Stressed Sex: Uncovering the Truth about Men, Women, and Mental Health*

★ *Anxiety: A Very Short Introduction*

★ *You Can Be Happy: The Scientifically Proven Way to Change How You Feel*

★ *Use Your Head: A Guided Tour of the Human Mind*

★ *Know Your Mind: The Complete Family Reference Guide to Emotional Health*

★ *Paranoia: The 21st-Century Fear*

★ *Overcoming Paranoid and Suspicious Thoughts*

Their work has appeared in various national newspapers and magazines, among them *The Times*, *The Guardian*, *The Independent* and *Psychologies*.

ACKNOWLEDGEMENTS

We are very grateful to our excellent publishing team at Pearson: Rachael Stock, who commissioned *How to Keep Calm and Carry On*, our editor Samantha Jackson, Lucy Carter and Emma Devlin. Thanks too, as ever, to our agent, Zoe King, at the Blair Partnership, for her encouragement, support and wise advice.

The personal accounts featured in this book are not direct quotations from actual individuals. They are illustrations of problems based upon diagnostic criteria and examples.

PUBLISHER'S ACKNOWLEDGEMENTS

We are grateful to the following for permission to reproduce copyright material:

Table on page 23 © NHS Health Scotland, University of Warwick and University of Edinburgh, 2006, all rights reserved; questionnaire on page 49 reprinted from *Behaviour Research and Therapy*, 28(6), Meyer, T.J., Miller, M.L., Metzger, R.L. and Borkovec, T.D., 'Development and validation of the Penn State Worry Questionnaire', pp. 487–95, © 1990, with permission from Elsevier.

In some instances we have been unable to trace the owners of copyright material, and we would appreciate any information that would enable us to do so.

PREFACE

Is anxiety becoming a nuisance for you? Do you find yourself worrying more than you used to? Are your fears getting you down? Are they starting to interfere with your day-to-day life?

If you've answered yes to any of these questions, you're in very good company. Anxiety is a problem that increasing numbers of us seem to be facing.

In one recent survey, for example, more than a third of UK adults reported feeling more anxious and fearful than they had in the past. Over three-quarters felt that the world had become a more frightening place over the previous decade. And almost a third said that anxiety had affected the way they lived their lives.

At the relatively severe end of the spectrum, anxiety disorders are (with depression) the most common form of psychological problem. Some surveys have found that as many as one in five people may have experienced an anxiety disorder – such as a phobia, panic attacks or obsessive-compulsive disorder – in the previous 12 months.

But although so many of us are struggling with our fears and worries, there is good news. Over recent years anxiety has been the focus of much cutting-edge psychological research. The treatments that have emerged from that research have been thoroughly tested in large-scale clinical trials. And the results of those trials are clear: these techniques really work.

In this book, we'll show you how to use those techniques to overcome your anxiety. As we know from our own clinical practice, they have helped many thousands of people and we are confident that they will help you, too.

Although it's based on the best scientific research, *How to Keep Calm and Carry On* is very much a practical book. You won't have to wade through lots of jargon-heavy theoretical stuff. What you'll find here are the techniques that will truly make a difference.

You may be surprised at how simple and straightforward these techniques often are. They may not be complex, but they are certainly effective. They will help you to free yourself from anxiety. You will feel more relaxed, more content and better able to cope with the challenges that life throws at you.

When we're very stressed or worried or anxious, it's easy to assume that there's nothing we can do to feel better – that we just have to endure the tough times. But we have far more control than we think. We can change our mood. We can overcome our anxiety. We can *keep calm and carry on*.

CHAPTER 1

What is anxiety?

'Keep calm and carry on' has become an extremely popular slogan in recent years. But it's a saying that goes right back to the early days of the Second World War.

In 1939, the UK Ministry of Information produced a series of three posters. One warned citizens: 'Freedom is in peril. Defend it with all your might.' A second proclaimed: '*Your* courage, *your* cheerfulness, *your* resolution will bring us victory.' And the third looked like this:

As it happens, this reassuring message wasn't seen by most people during the war because the poster wasn't widely distributed. But there can't be many of us who haven't come across it in recent years!

Why has it become so popular? Well, first of all it's a slogan that recognises that we all find life stressful sometimes. (And with the global economy in its current precarious state, many of us may feel we have more to worry about than in previous, less nerve-wracking times.)

Second, and most importantly, the poster offers us some pretty good advice. It's so good, in fact, that we've chosen it as the title of this book. Anxiety will come and go – it's only natural – but we don't have to let it get the better of us. We can master our worries and fears. We can learn to *keep calm and carry on.*

In the coming pages, we'll show you how. There's no mystery. You don't have to be a particular kind of person. The techniques you'll discover have all been subjected to rigorous scientific testing. They aren't 'wishful thinking'. They aren't simply a nice theory. They are backed up by hard science.

We use these techniques every day in our clinical practice. Many thousands of people – people with all kinds of backgrounds, talents and worries – have found them helpful. They worked for these individuals and they can work for you, too.

Here's another slogan for you: *knowledge is power.* It's a phrase that, in one form or another, has been around for thousands of years – which is a pretty good indication of its wisdom.

What it means, at least in part, is that we have a much better chance of accomplishing our objective if we understand what it involves. We gather information and then take action. Whether choosing a new mobile phone, deciding which evening class you're going to take, or picking a restaurant for Friday night, your decision will be all the better for some research. And dealing with your worries and fears is no different.

That's why the first chapter in this book is devoted to the question: *what is anxiety?* We're not going to subject you to an exhaustive academic discussion of the topic. What we're going to give you are the key facts.

Why not jump straight into the practical techniques? After all, they're probably the main reason why you've picked up this book. Well, we think you'll get the most out of those techniques if you see where they're coming from – if you understand what anxiety is and why it affects us in the way it does. Remember: knowledge is power.

Imagine a life without worry, without fear, without stress. Wouldn't it be wonderful?

And have you ever flicked through the pages of a magazine – one of those crammed with pictures of tanned and beaming celebrities – and thought to yourself: *Those people have nothing to worry about. Their lives are just one long holiday. I wish it were me!*

In fact, you can bet your bottom dollar that those celebrities experience their share of anxiety. How do we know? Because it's an emotion that everyone feels at least sometimes. *Everyone.* That means you, your best friend, your boss, your neighbours, the people you see on TV (yes, including the ones with the 'perfect' bodies and shiny hair) – heck, even the authors of this book.

We might, for instance, feel anxious when we meet new people, or when we have to give a presentation at work.

We might be scared of heights, certain types of animal, or the sight of blood. We might worry that we're going to develop a serious illness. Maybe we've had a fright and are finding it difficult to move on: perhaps, for example, we've been involved in a traffic accident and are now fearful of travelling by car. Or perhaps we find ourselves spending far more time than we'd like fretting about potential problems.

Whatever is troubling you, remember that anxiety is normal and natural. We all experience it – and especially perhaps when we're feeling stressed, tired, ill or run down. And sometimes anxiety can be essential. We might dream about a life without anxiety, but in reality we need it – occasionally, at least.

Why? What's so great about anxiety? Wouldn't we all be much better off without it?

Maybe we should ask the dodo. This unfortunate creature lived quite happily for many centuries on the uninhabited island of Mauritius. Then one day humans arrived, and more specifically hungry sailors – with guns. The dodo, having never seen these strange creatures before, wasn't scared. It didn't run away (it couldn't fly). And within a hundred years, the dodo was extinct. So much for fearlessness.

> *Anxiety is an emotion, and like all emotions it has a purpose.*

Anxiety is an emotion, and like all emotions it has a purpose. Happiness, for instance, marks out the experiences it's beneficial for us to repeat. Feeling sad helps point us away from unhelpful situations. And anxiety is our early warning system. It alerts us to potential danger and gives us the chance to decide how we're going to respond.

Perhaps you've come across the phrase 'fight or flight'. It was coined in 1915 by an American professor of physiology, Walter Cannon. It describes how animals mostly behave when they feel anxiety or fear (the two words are pretty much interchangeable): either they run or they confront the threat head on.

This was probably the case for our ancestors, too. But for modern humans, things tend to be a little more complicated. For a start, the kinds of worries we face are often far more subtle than whether or not we'll be attacked by a predator. And we're also capable of a much greater range of responses to anxiety than animals. We can pretend we don't feel it, for example: *What? Me anxious? Not at all! I'm fine. Honestly, I am ...*

Yet many of our reactions to anxiety can still be seen as examples of fight or flight. Perhaps, for example, we're worried about attending a party because it means spending the evening with new people. In fact, we feel so anxious that we opt to stay at home: that's flight. Or imagine that we're walking through a crowded shopping centre. Suddenly we feel a bump from behind and turn around to see a figure dashing away with our wallet in his hand. Though we are shaking with fear, we give chase, rugby tackle the robber to the floor and wrest the wallet from his hand: this is fight.

Actually, there's a third kind of reaction that animals tend to use when frightened: freezing. Cat owners may well have observed this response up close (we certainly have). Hearing a manic clattering and scurrying, you head downstairs and discover your cat with some kind of rodent. When the unfortunate animal tries to escape, the cat instantly leaps on it in a frenzy of excitement. But when the rodent stays very still, the cat is bemused and often – and much to your relief – quickly loses interest. We humans may also freeze when very anxious. You may have experienced it yourself: *I was so scared I couldn't move …*

But whether we fight, flee, freeze or pick some entirely different option, the point is that we can all choose how we react to anxiety.

Inevitably there will be times when it's right to be anxious, when we need to listen to our fear and deal with the threat that's facing us. Imagine that you're busy cooking your evening meal. You're chopping vegetables and humming along to a song on the radio. Suddenly, out of the corner of your eye, you see the oil in the frying pan burst into flames. Anxiety spurs you into immediate action. Instantly you stop what you've been doing and hurry over to the cooker. You don't hear the radio any more. You are totally focused on the job in hand. And just as well, too.

But there are also times when our anxiety is misplaced, when we find ourselves fretting about trivialities or maybe even feeling on edge or panicky without knowing why. Maybe it seems as though these times are the norm for you. Little hassles have a nasty habit of appearing to be big problems. Life is exhaustingly stressful. You may feel as though you're different from other people: less confident and more vulnerable; somehow not up to the task. You may wonder: *Why can't I cope like everyone else?* Worrying takes up far too much of your time and energy. And you want it to change.

It's this second kind of anxiety – the unhelpful, unjustified, exaggerated kind – that this book is designed to tackle. It might seem difficult to believe right now, but it truly is possible to take control of those fears and worries. You don't need them; they serve no useful purpose. Can you feel calmer, more content, more confident about life? If you put into practice even a few of the techniques we set out in the following chapters, you'll find that the answer to that question is: *Yes, I can.*

Let's take a more detailed look at how anxiety works. Scientists have discovered that it affects us on three basic levels:

- ★ Our thoughts
- ★ Our body
- ★ Our behaviour.

OUR THOUGHTS

The first of these three, our thoughts, we can call the *psychological* level. In the heat of the moment, as we realise we're driving too fast to make it round the hairpin bend, thoughts race through our mind: *Uh oh! I've misjudged this. I'm going to be in trouble if I don't hit the brakes … right NOW!* These are called 'hot cognitions'. They're our immediate psychological response to potential danger. And they seem to spring into our consciousness automatically, pushing all other thoughts out of our mind.

But anxiety alters our thinking in many other ways. We worry about what might happen in the future. We worry about what's happened in the past (the psychological term for this is 'rumination'). We may even find ourselves worrying about the fact that we're worrying: *What does it mean? Am I going crazy? Will I never be able to stop?*

Unpleasant images may come to mind. We see ourselves giving tomorrow's presentation at work; observe the expressions of boredom on the faces of our audience; notice with horror that we're stumbling over our words, sweat dripping into our eyes, hands trembling so violently that the notes we're holding bounce up and down like a toddler on a trampoline.

Unhappy memories keep making their presence felt. We remember the bad times and forget the good. What about that occasion a few years back when our neighbour felt a bit tired and breathless after a walk in the countryside and it turned out he needed major heart surgery? Or the plane flight we spent worrying whether the engines were going to fail? Or the time last year when our boss wondered whether we ought not to have spent just a little longer working on that report before submitting it? What if these sorts of thing happen again? How will we cope?

And when we're in stressful situations our thoughts centre on how we're feeling, how well we're performing whatever task it is and what people might be thinking of us. When we go to a party, we're instantly on edge. Is our heart racing? How does our stomach feel? Are we sweating? And can the other guests see how nervous we are? Did we say something stupid? Are we making a really poor impression? And, most importantly, how soon can we leave?

OUR BODY

Anxiety produces a series of changes in our body, each of them designed to help us deal with whatever threat is facing us. (This is what we might call the *physiological* level of anxiety.) These changes are fine if we really are in danger, but much less useful when we're not.

These physical changes occur because of anxiety's effect on our nervous system, and specifically what's known as the autonomic nervous system or ANS. The job of the ANS is to look after the basic physiological processes such as breathing, blood pressure and keeping the body at the right temperature. When we feel fear, the sympathetic nervous system (SNS), a subsystem of the ANS, takes over. And another subsystem, the parasympathetic nervous system (PNS), steps in when it's time to calm down.

So, for example, the sympathetic nervous system makes our heart beat faster, allowing blood to reach our muscles more rapidly (by as much as 1,200 per cent in some cases). We're primed for action. The digestive system is put on hold, so that the body can focus all its energies on dealing with the possible danger. One of the side effects is that we produce less saliva, which explains why lots of people experience a dry mouth when they're anxious. And the pupils widen, relaxing the lens and allowing more light to reach the eye. Indeed, new research suggests that the facial expression people typically assume when frightened – eyes wide open, nostrils flared, eyebrows raised – actually helps us to see better and to detect scents more efficiently. If we're stuck in a dangerous situation, these changes could make all the difference.

OUR BEHAVIOUR

The physical effects of anxiety feel pretty unpleasant – so unpleasant in fact that they're virtually impossible to ignore. Our heart races, our mouth dries, our stomach churns. And, of course, anxious thoughts aren't much fun either.

And that's the point. Anxiety is potentially life-saving, so we can't afford not to notice it. Because it feels horrible, we want it to stop as quickly as possible. It's intended to function like a very sharp stick, prodding us into action: to bring about a change in our *behaviour*.

One of the most basic ways our behaviour alters is in our posture. We tense up, on edge for whatever might happen next. We hunch over, as if to protect ourselves from danger.

> *Anxiety can gee us up, focusing our mind and body on the job in hand.*

Actors and sports stars often talk about the nerves they need to feel in order to perform at peak level. Anxiety can gee us up, focusing our mind and body on the job in hand: it's the 'fight' response channelled in a healthier direction. This is another reminder that anxiety isn't always bad news. We may not like it, but sometimes we need it.

But of course anxiety is such an unpleasant feeling that many of us would go to great lengths not to experience it! And so our behaviour can revolve around *avoiding* (or fleeing) those troubling thoughts and nasty sensations.

Take Alex, for instance. Alex finds meeting new people stressful and he'll generally try to give those situations a miss. Sometimes, however, he can't get out of it. A couple of months ago, his wife threw a big party to celebrate her sister's fortieth birthday. Alex knew that there was no way he could avoid this particular event, and in fact he quite wanted to go. Yet when he scanned the guest list and carefully totted up the names, he realised that he would know only about a quarter of the guests. *I'm going to really struggle here,* he thought to himself. *I might end up not speaking to anyone. I'll be standing around on my own like a spare part.* The thought, understandably, made him anxious, and that feeling grew as the day of the party approached. *I wish I didn't have to do this,* he found himself thinking again and again.

But over the years Alex had developed a number of strategies to use in situations like this. So he spent most of the evening in the company of people he already knew well. If someone new joined the group, he would let other people do the talking. When he did make a comment, his overriding objective was to make sure that no one could possibly be offended. He constantly tried to gauge how he was coming across. And when Alex was finding things tough, he would quietly slip out for a while.

These kinds of strategies are known as *safety behaviours.* People use them because they think they'll prevent what they fear from occurring. Safety behaviours can certainly reduce anxiety in the short term. But we don't discover that, without them, we're actually in no great danger. And so in the long run they only increase our fears. We'll hear a lot more about safety behaviours in Chapter 3.

Perhaps you recognise something of Alex in your own behaviour. Do you try to avoid situations that make you anxious? If you're unable to avoid them, do you find yourself using safety behaviours to cope? And when you feel anxiety building, do you try to escape?

Because anxiety affects us psychologically, physically and behaviourally, making a positive change on just *one* of these levels is enough for us to notice an improvement.

The very best way to master anxiety, however, is to tackle all three levels. That may sound wildly ambitious. But in fact it's what the best therapy is designed to achieve. And you can achieve it, too.

In recent years, clinical psychologists have developed very powerful techniques that build on the insight that the three levels are interconnected. This means that if you make the right kinds of changes to your thoughts, for example, you can alter both your response to the physical signs of anxiety and your behaviour.

We'll talk you through these techniques. We'll show you how to make these changes. You'll discover that you can alter the way you think, how you feel and how you behave. And when you do that, you'll find that you are far calmer and much less anxious.

CHAPTER 2

Why you really can overcome your anxiety

When we're struggling with anxiety, we may feel as if things will never improve. We don't know why we're fearful in certain situations, and we may find it hard to remember a time when we weren't plagued by anxiety.

So we assume, for example, that we'll always be scared of heights; that we'll never be confident about speaking in public; or that meeting new people will always be stressful for us. *That's just the way I am*, we tell ourselves.

But it isn't so. We aren't doomed to be anxious all our life. We can change. We can learn to cope with the situations that worry us, and even to face them with confidence. In this chapter we'll find out why.

Imagine that you were asked to write a description of yourself. What would you include? You might mention your age, where you live, whether you're married or have children, what you do for a living, your physical appearance, your interests and hobbies. But do these details capture the real you?

Yes and no, you might think. For sure, things like our family ties, our work and our age are all important pieces in the puzzle of who we are. But most of us feel that there's more to us than just these 'facts'. This kind of information, we think, doesn't say anything much about what we're like deep down.

So how do we describe our 'inner' self? Well, we might talk about how we see the world, and our place within it. We might mention our values – the things that are important to us. What are our aspirations, our strengths and weaknesses? How do we relate to other people? How do we conduct ourselves? Are we outgoing or shy, adventurous or wary, easy-going or self-disciplined?

Much of what we're getting at here is what we call our *person-ality*. And most of us tend to think that it's the unchanging core of our identity. Whatever else happens in our life, we assume, our personality will remain pretty much the same – because that's what we're like!

Philosophers and scientists have been thinking about person-ality for centuries. For a very long time – from the ancient Greeks right up until the nineteenth century – it was believed that our personality was a reflection of our biological make-up, and specifically the distribution in our body of something called 'humours'.

There were reckoned to be four humours: black bile, yellow bile, phlegm and blood. Your personality reflected the balance of these substances in your body. For example, bad-tempered people had too much yellow bile; sad people were suffering from an excess of black bile; very laid-back folk were supposedly full of phlegm.

You can see the traces of this theory in our language today – easy-going people are still sometimes referred to as 'phlegmatic' and irate types as 'choleric'. But that's about as far as it goes: there's no scientific evidence to back up the idea of humours.

These days psychologists take a very different approach. Rather than four humours, we think of five fundamental personality traits. The 'Big Five' are:

- ★ Openness (curious, imaginative, unconventional)
- ★ Conscientiousness (hard-working, goal-oriented, self-disciplined)
- ★ Extraversion (pleasure-seeking, adventurous, lively)
- ★ Agreeableness (helpful, kind, sensitive to the needs of others)
- ★ Neuroticism (anxious, nervous, pessimistic).

It's not all or nothing with the Big Five (to help you remember their names, you can use the mnemonic OCEAN). We aren't simply 'extravert' or 'open'. Instead we all have more or less of each trait. And it's that mixture that defines our personality. Indeed, although we all share these traits to a greater or lesser extent, that doesn't mean there are only a small number of possible personalities. In fact, one expert has estimated that there are around 100,000!

So how do the Big Five relate to anxiety? Well, you'll probably have noticed number five: neuroticism. The more of this particular personality trait people have, the more they tend to focus on the negative aspect of things, and the more keenly they feel the stresses and strains of life.

If there's a lot of neuroticism in our personality, does that mean we're bound to be more anxious than other people? Can we change our personality? Can we moderate its effects on the way we feel and behave?

Scientific research has shown that personality is partly influenced by our genes. But the key word to remember here is 'partly'. Though we're used to thinking about personality as somehow innate, in fact it isn't – or at least only to a limited degree.

What's at least as important – and probably more so – are our life experiences: the people we spend time with, the places we go to, the things that happen to us. This is what psychologists call *environment* and there's no doubt that it plays a huge role in determining the kind of person we are.

Discovering that our personality isn't simply something we're born with may seem a bit disorienting at first, perhaps even a little scary. *Maybe if things had happened differently when I was a child*, we might think, *I wouldn't be me. Perhaps I'd be someone else entirely.*

We aren't 'born worriers'. We don't have to put up with our anxiety. We can overcome it.

It's a dizzying thought. But it's also wonderfully liberating. Because it means that we don't just have to shrug our shoulders and make do with whatever personality traits life has landed us with. We aren't 'born worriers'. We don't have to put up with our anxiety. We can overcome it.

This doesn't mean the slate is totally blank. We're not just the sum of our experiences. Genes have *something* to say about our personality. But they don't decide it. Instead we can think of them as boundary markers: they set out the limits of what's possible. And those markers are pretty far apart, leaving lots of latitude for us to shape the kind of person we want to become.

What kinds of life events make people anxious? Where do our fears come from?

Well, there's lots of evidence that anxiety – like so much of our behaviour – is *learned*. One of the most famous psychological experiments ever conducted made just this point.

The experiment took place in London in 1920. The American psychologist John B. Watson and his assistant Rosalie Rayner set out to discover whether they could teach a nine-month-old boy, known as 'Albert B.', to be afraid of certain objects.

(You might be raising your eyebrows at this point. *Surely scientists shouldn't be going around scaring young children?* You're right: they shouldn't. But at the time Watson and Rayner were working, ethics committees were unheard of. Their experiment would never get the green light these days.)

Here's how Watson and Rayner went about teaching little Albert to be afraid. First of all they showed Albert a white rat, a rabbit, a dog, cotton wool and burning newspapers. None of these troubled him in the slightest. Albert was an easy-going, happy chap and not the type to scare easily.

However, a few weeks later Watson and Rayner showed Albert the white rat again. And this time, as soon as Albert reached out to touch the animal, the psychologists slammed a hammer against a steel bar, producing a sudden and frighteningly loud noise.

Over the next few weeks, the psychologists discovered that Albert was now afraid of the white rat, even when the steel bar wasn't struck. And not only that: he was also scared of objects that looked a bit like the rat, such as a rabbit or even Watson's hair.

What does this tell us? Well, Watson and Rayner argued that baby Albert's experience is typical of us all. We come into the world relatively free of fears and learn them, usually in childhood.

It's not necessary for a scary event to happen to us personally. We pick up many of our fears from the people around us. If your dad tells you repeatedly that dogs are dangerous, there's a good chance you might grow up believing that they genuinely are a potential hazard, even though you may never have actually seen them hurting anyone.

We can learn to be anxious even without explicit warnings from other people. Sometimes just *observing* their behaviour is enough. And for most of us, no one is more influential than our parents – though we can certainly learn our fears from other important adults in our life, and also from our friends.

For a fascinating demonstration of the power parents have to influence their children's emotions, we can turn to an experiment carried out a few years back by Friederike Gerull and Ronald Rapee. They showed 30 Australian toddlers a green rubber snake and then a purple rubber spider, and studied their reactions.

While the toys were on display, the children's mothers were asked to react in a happy and encouraging way or in a frightened or disgusted manner. Later, the snake and the spider were shown to the toddlers a couple of times more, though on these occasions their mothers' reactions were strictly neutral.

Gerull and Rapee noticed that you could predict how a child would react to the toy when they saw it again. It was simple: the child copied the mother's response. If the mother had pretended to be afraid, the child was frightened. If the mother had appeared calm and happy, the toddler reacted in the same way.

This process is called 'modelling'. And it plays a big part in how we acquire our fears.

Now, the fact that so much of our anxiety is learned is very good news for us all. Why? Because it shows that things can be different. We aren't *naturally* worried and fearful. We've just learned to be that way.

That's all well and good, you might counter, but I have those fears and worries now. I can hardly unlearn them, can I?

Yes, you can. Your anxiety doesn't reflect the way the world is; it reflects the way you *see* the world. And just as you learned these beliefs, you can replace them with other, more positive beliefs. What has been learned can be *un*learned.

What's happening in our brain when we feel anxiety?

Thanks to the pioneering work of US neuroscientist Joseph LeDoux, we now know that one region of the brain in particular seems to be crucial. That region is called the 'amygdala', two small pieces of tissue that early scientists thought looked like almond seeds (*amygdala* is the Latin term for 'almond seed').

(As well as being a professor at New York University's Center for Neural Research, LeDoux is vocalist and guitarist with The Amygdaloids, a rock band specialising in 'songs about love and life peppered with insights drawn from research about mind and brain and mental disorders'.)

The amygdala is a storehouse of unconscious emotional memories. If we've felt frightened in a particular situation, the amygdala will remember. And it uses these memories to judge whether we're in danger now. If it thinks we are, we feel anxious. And the purpose of anxiety (as we saw in Chapter 1) is to alert us to potential trouble and equip us to deal with it.

The amygdala makes its judgements extremely rapidly. It's much quicker than our conscious thoughts. In fact, it's so speedy that we may not know why we're suddenly feeling anxious.

Now the fact that the amygdala operates at such lightning speed brings both advantages and disadvantages.

On the plus side, it means that we can respond to danger really quickly. LeDoux calls it a 'quick and dirty' reaction that's designed to save our life first and ask questions later.

Imagine you're crossing the road one night. Out of nowhere, a car roars around the bend towards you. Now, you could make a considered judgement as to whether, given your current pace and the speed of the car, you're really about to be run over. But the car is moving so fast, and it's so difficult to see clearly in the dark, that you don't have time to make a conscious decision. Instinctively, and with your heart pumping frantically, you leap backwards. And the car rushes past.

On this occasion, the speed of the amygdala may well have saved your life. But because it reacts so quickly, the amygdala can make mistakes. It can sometimes exaggerate the danger we're in, or even detect threats in safe situations. And that means we feel anxious when we don't need to.

Scientists think that anxious people may possess a hyperactive amygdala. (Or as the journalist Jon Ronson put it: 'I imagined my amygdala to be like one of those Hubble photographs of a solar storm.') Maybe this is because of the experiences they've had in their lives and the fears they've learned. And possibly it's the result of genetic factors.

> *Even if your amygdala is livelier than you might like, it can be calmed.*

But even if your amygdala is livelier than you might like, it can be calmed. As you learn to conquer your anxiety, you reset your amygdala. It's like repairing a faulty fire alarm – you need it to go off when there's a genuine cause for concern, not each time you stick a piece of bread in the toaster.

How do we sort out our overactive amygdala? We re-educate it. We replace its anxious memories with positive ones. We learn that the situation we fear is in fact safe.

How exactly we go about this learning process has been the subject of much cutting-edge psychological research in recent years. The techniques that have emerged from this research have been tested repeatedly in large-scale clinical trials. And the evidence is clear: they really do produce significant reductions in anxiety. They lead to positive changes in the brain. And they help people to feel calmer, more confident, happier.

If you're reading this book, the chances are you want to improve the way you feel. You want to take control of your worries and fears. You want to regain composure, calmness, contentment.

Is it possible? Absolutely. As you put into practice the techniques in this book, your mood will steadily change for the better.

You can track this improvement. As soon as it's convenient for you, fill in the following questionnaire. It's been designed to pinpoint how happy you're feeling right now.

Over the coming weeks, fill in the questionnaire again. It'll show you just how far you've come. We think you'll be pleasantly surprised.

THE WARWICK–EDINBURGH MENTAL WELL-BEING SCALE

When you answer the questions opposite, base your answers on how you've been feeling over the past fortnight.

Then add up your scores: first for each of the columns and then for the columns combined. The higher your score, the happier you probably are. The average score, incidentally, is approximately 50 out of 70.

	None of the time	Rarely	Some of the time	Often	All of the time
I've been feeling optimistic about the future	☐ 1	☐ 2	☑ 3	☐ 4	☐ 5
I've been feeling useful	☑ 1	☐ 2	☐ 3	☐ 4	☐ 5
I've been feeling relaxed	☑ 1	☐ 2	☐ 3	☐ 4	☐ 5
I've been feeling interested in other people	☐ 1	☑ 2	☐ 3	☐ 4	☐ 5
I've had energy to spare	☑ 1	☐ 2	☐ 3	☐ 4	☐ 5
I've been dealing with problems well	☐ 1	☑ 2	☐ 3	☐ 4	☐ 5
I've been thinking clearly	☑ 1	☐ 2	☐ 3	☐ 4	☐ 5
I've been feeling good about myself	☑ 1	☐ 2	☐ 3	☐ 4	☐ 5
I've been feeling close to other people	☐ 1	☑ 2	☐ 3	☐ 4	☐ 5
I've been feeling confident	☑ 1	☐ 2	☐ 3	☐ 4	☐ 5
I've been able to make up my own mind about things	☐ 1	☑ 2	☐ 3	☐ 4	☐ 5
I've been feeling loved	☐ 1	☐ 2	☑ 3	☐ 4	☐ 5
I've been interested in new things	☐ 1	☑ 2	☐ 3	☐ 4	☐ 5
I've been feeling cheerful	☑ 1	☐ 2	☐ 3	☐ 4	☐ 5
Scores	7	10	6		
Total score	23				

CHAPTER 3

Tackling anxious thoughts

In this chapter we're going to learn how to deal with one of the most important drivers of anxiety: our thoughts.

Did you know that the average person experiences more than 4,000 thoughts a day? 4,000! Most of them pop into – and out of – our minds without any conscious effort. They seem to appear from nowhere and usually within a few moments we've forgotten they were ever there.

The vast majority of our thoughts come and go and leave scarcely a trace. They aren't important. And yet we don't tend to see it like this. Instead, we attach huge significance to our thoughts. We assume they *mean* something. We believe that they tell us something useful about ourselves and the world around us.

Sometimes, of course, they do. Sometimes our thoughts are carefully considered. They're based on good evidence. They are, in other words, genuinely *thoughtful*. But how many of those 4,000 daily thoughts are like this? Most of the time, hardly any.

Unfortunately, we don't tend to be all that good at distinguishing the significant thoughts from the insignificant. And that can mean we end up believing things that, in a nutshell, just aren't true.

> *All too often our fears are based on thoughts and beliefs that aren't reliable guides to future events.*

This can be a real problem when it comes to anxiety. All too often our fears are based on thoughts and beliefs that aren't reliable guides to future events. We may *think* we're going to come to harm, but the reality is often very different. Winston Churchill put it nicely: 'When I look back on all these worries, I remember the story of the old man who said on his deathbed that he had had a lot of trouble in his life, most of which had never happened.'

Emily is 32 and a charity fund-raiser. She's nervous about heights. Here are some of the thoughts that go through her head when it looks as though she might have to climb beyond her comfort zone: *I'm going to trip and fall. What if I suddenly decide to jump? Everyone will see how anxious I am and they'll think that I'm nuts.*

Rob, a 40-year-old computer programmer, finds it difficult to leave the house unless he has checked repeatedly that the doors and windows are closed and all his gas and electrical appliances are turned off. *One day I'm bound to leave the cooker on, or the back door unlocked. We'll be burgled, or the house will burn down. And it'll be my fault.*

Helen, a retired shop manager, is anxious about speaking in public. *I'm no good at it. I'm bound to forget what I want to say. I'll stutter over my words. People will see how jittery I am and they'll think I'm weak and silly.*

What anxious thoughts do you have? Jot them down on a piece of paper. There's no need to go into lots of detail – a few simple bullet points will do just fine.

To help you remember, think back to a recent time when you felt anxious. Close your eyes if you like and try to visualise the moment in as much detail as you can. What was going through your mind? What did you fear might happen? Were there particular thoughts that you couldn't shake off – worries that kept reappearing in your mind?

Here's an example from Alex (who we met in Chapter 1). Alex becomes anxious in social situations, and especially when he's meeting new people. He remembers the thoughts that filled his mind when he discovered that his wife was planning a big birthday party for her sister:

★ *I can't do this.*

★ *I won't know most of the guests and I'll end up standing on my own.*

★ *I'm no good at making small talk. I'll feel out of place.*

★ *Everyone will notice how anxious I am and they'll keep well away.*

Of course, there's one very effective way to identify your anxious thoughts – and that's to actually experience the situation you find stressful. If you feel up to it, you could consciously seek out that situation. Think of it as a research expedition: if I walk past that dog, or take the lift to the top floor, or strike up a conversation with someone I don't know well, what thoughts enter my mind?

If this kind of 'field trip' doesn't appeal, try to notice what you're thinking the next time you feel worried or anxious or stressed. And when you get a moment, write down those thoughts.

It's really important to identify exactly what it is about the situation that worries you. What do you believe is going to happen? What harm do you fear?

You might find that it takes a little digging to unearth these thoughts. Often when we're anxious all we can think is: *This is awful. I have to get out of here.* But we have to go deeper. We have to work out what makes the situation seem so awful. We have to identify why we're so desperate to get away. In most cases it boils down to one or more of three basic scenarios:

1 I'll lose control – I'll go mad, say things I don't mean, or faint.

2 I'll be humiliated in front of other people.

3 I'll be in physical danger.

Alex's anxiety stemmed from the second of these. He was afraid that somehow he wouldn't come up to scratch at the party and that the other guests would think badly of him for it. Which of the three scenarios lies at the root of your own anxiety?

You may be wondering why it's so important to identify our anxious thoughts. What does it matter? How does it help?

Well, those thoughts are absolutely central to our anxiety. As we saw in Chapter 1, anxiety is all about the anticipation of threat. We judge that we're somehow in danger. And that anticipation, that judgement, happens via our thoughts. We *think* we're going to be bitten by the approaching dog and that's why we feel anxious.

But what if these thoughts are wrong? What if our anxiety is based on a mistaken estimate of the risks we face in a particular situation? *What if there's really nothing to worry about?* Imagine how wonderfully liberating that would be!

For example, many people with phobias believe that coming into contact with whatever it is they fear will cause them to faint. At the root of their anxiety is the first of the scenarios we described opposite: the idea that they'll lose control.

But it can't happen. Their anxiety is based on an untrue thought. Fainting happens when our blood pressure plummets. When we're anxious, however, our blood pressure increases, making fainting an impossibility.

(There is one exception: people with a phobia of blood, injections and injuries can experience a drop in blood pressure. Experts don't know for sure why this occurs, but it makes sense. Lowered blood pressure doesn't only cause us to faint, it also reduces the flow of blood around the body. And that just might save your life if you did happen to be badly wounded.)

> *It's time to turn the tables. It's time to shake up your preconceptions.*

Perhaps you've fallen into the habit of taking your anxious thoughts on trust. And maybe those thoughts are misleading. Perhaps they're triggering an anxiety that there's no good reason for you to feel. But it's time to turn the tables. It's time to shake up your preconceptions. And you can't do that unless you have a clear sense of the thoughts you're going to investigate.

★ ★ ★ ★ ★ ★

All being well, you now have a list of your anxious thoughts. How exactly do you go about finding out whether or not they're accurate? How do you put them to the test?

The key is to place yourself in the situations that spark the thoughts. That might sound scary. You might think: *When I'm in this sort of situation in everyday life I get anxious. So how is it suddenly going to help me deal with my anxiety?*

The answer is that you're going to take things steadily. You're not just throwing yourself into stressful situations. You're going to carry out a carefully planned behavioural test. And you can be certain that, when you've finished, you will be much less anxious than you are now.

In a moment we'll talk through how to design and carry out your own behavioural test. But first we need to let you know about one crucial ground rule.

Here it is: when you expose yourself to the situations that make you anxious, you must *let go of your safety behaviours.*

What is a safety behaviour? Well, as we saw in Chapter 1, it's an action we take in order to prevent whatever we're afraid of from happening. We have an anxious thought (*If I'm up high I will somehow fall to my death*) and we adopt a safety behaviour to stop that thought turning into reality (*I'll keep away from heights*). First comes the thought, then the behaviour follows.

Safety behaviours take three forms. The first is called *avoidance* and it's what we do when we steer clear of the situation we fear – as in our example about heights.

The second is *escape*: if we find ourselves in that situation, we get out of there as quickly as we can. Maybe a friend has persuaded me to climb up the bell tower of a picturesque church. But no sooner have I reached the top than I'm hurrying back down again.

The third form is *within-situation* safety behaviours. As you'll guess from the name, these are the actions we take while we're in the situation that makes us anxious. So, for example, when I'm up high I try to stay well away from the edge. I keep close to other people. And I never, ever look down!

Alex uses all three kinds of safety behaviour. He avoids social situations where he might have to meet lots of new people. If this proves impossible (as it did for his sister-in-law's birthday party), he likes to leave early.

While he's at the event, Alex tries to stick with people he already knows. With new people, he can't relax. Instead he constantly monitors how he's coming across. He tries to avoid making eye contact in case the other person can see how anxious he is. He holds his wine glass tightly to stop his hands from shaking. And because he fears he'll say something silly or stumble over his words, he mentally rehearses his comments – in fact, Alex probably pays more attention to the conversation he's planning in his mind than the one he's actually having with the person he's talking to.

Taking action to avoid danger is perfectly reasonable – our life might depend on it. But safety behaviours aren't helpful when our fears are unrealistic. This is because they deprive us of the opportunity to put our anxiety to the test. When what we fear doesn't occur, we assume it's because of our safety behaviours. And we overlook the simplest explanation: the problem actually wasn't very likely in the first place. We don't confront what we fear and therefore we aren't able to discover that our worries are misplaced.

There's also good evidence that within-situation safety behaviours actually *increase* our anxiety. Alex, for example, isn't calmed by his constant self-monitoring. He feels worse, probably because all his attention is focused on his fears. He can't let himself go and simply enjoy the occasion.

Not only that, but Alex's safety behaviours do nothing to improve his performance; in reality, they hamper it. His conversation seems stilted. His constant grip on his wine glass betrays his anxiety. And his unwillingness to look people in the face can come across as unfriendly. In fact, these behaviours run the risk of producing exactly the kinds of problems Alex is so desperate to avoid.

Spend some time now listing your own safety behaviours. What tactics do you use to get you through those stressful moments? Do you opt for avoidance or escape? Which within-situation safety behaviours do you tend to employ?

Because our anxiety isn't challenged, it can grow ever stronger. It's like a weed in the garden: you can cut it back or try to cover it up with other plants, and that will work for a short while. But the only way to get rid of it for good is to take it out by the roots – that is, by tackling our anxious thoughts. No half measures!

We're going to show you now how to challenge those thoughts by conducting your own behavioural test. There are six steps:

★ Step 1 is to choose the anxious thought you're going to test and to rate how strongly you believe that thought, from 0 per cent to 100 per cent.

★ Step 2 is to think of a situation that will allow you to test the thought.

★ Step 3 is to identify the safety behaviours you normally use when you have this anxious thought. These are the safety behaviours you'll need to drop during the test.

★ Step 4 is to think of any problems that might make it difficult for you to carry out the test.

★ Step 5 is to carry out the test and to observe what happens.

★ Step 6 is to assess how you feel about your negative thought now. How strongly do you believe it after the test, from 0 per cent to 100 per cent?

This is the behavioural test Alex carried out:

★ Step 1: Anxious thought is that when I chat to people who I don't know I'll be so nervous and tongue-tied that they'll get away from me as fast as they can. Believe this 95 per cent.

★ Step 2: Aim to talk to at least one new person at Liz's party.

★ Step 3: Will need to attend party; won't keep checking my watch to see when I can leave; mustn't avoid new people; won't rehearse what I'm going to say; will make eye contact.

★ Step 4: I guess the main problems might be that I'm too anxious to approach a new person, or that no one will come over to speak to me.

★ Step 5: Managed to have conversations with three people I'd never met before! Was really stressed beforehand and nervous at the start of each chat. But it seemed to go quite well. I was able to get the words out. I even made a few jokes! And I didn't feel that any of the people were keen to stop talking to me. In fact, one of them admitted that he'd been a bit worried that he wouldn't know anyone and said that he was really pleased to have met me!

★ Step 6: Perhaps I was just lucky with the people I met. But maybe I'm not as bad at socialising as I think. Rate the thought at 50 per cent now.

When you carry out your behavioural test, you'll probably feel anxious. You might find that your heart is racing, your body is trembling and your stomach is performing somersaults. That's perfectly normal. But you'll discover that these physical sensations don't mean anything. They aren't signs of impending disaster. They're simply a reaction to your thoughts – and your thoughts aren't as reliable as they once seemed.

Anxiety, remember, is learned. Generally speaking, we aren't born with our fears. No one comes out of the womb afraid of public speaking! Our anxiety is largely created by the experiences that we have during our life. And because it's learned, it can be unlearned.

When we test out our anxious thoughts in a behavioural experiment we discover that those thoughts are inaccurate. Our fears are based on a misconception. We believed we were in danger, but in reality we are safe.

CHAPTER 4

More ways to tackle anxious thoughts

You have probably noticed that the title of this chapter is rather similar to that of the previous one. But it really is worth spending more time learning how to combat anxious thoughts. Because thoughts play an absolutely central part in anxiety.

As we saw in Chapter 2, one of the fundamental insights of recent psychological research is that troublesome anxiety is a response to an imagined future threat, and not actual current danger. How we *interpret* events can be much more important than those events themselves. In other words, it's what goes on in our head that matters.

Imagine that you're lying in bed at night, fast asleep. Suddenly you're woken by a noise downstairs. What could it be? If you decide that it's your cat crashing through the cat flap or knocking precious objects from shelves, you might feel cross but you'll probably turn over and go back to sleep – though you might be cursing as you do so.

But if you think the noise may have been made by a burglar, your reaction is bound to be very different. Instead of relaxing, you'll be instantly on edge. Anxious thoughts will flood your mind. Should you venture downstairs into who knows what kind of danger? Will you be attacked? Can you cope with what might happen? What if the intruder decides to come upstairs? Your heart may pound; your breathing suddenly becomes shallow; your stomach may churn. And even after you've come to the conclusion that you're probably not being burgled after all, you may feel so tense and agitated that falling back to sleep takes an age.

So you can see that exactly the same event is capable of triggering wildly different interpretations. If we're anxious it's because we're thinking anxious thoughts. And those thoughts determine how we feel and how we behave. All of which means that challenging our anxious thoughts should be our number-one priority. In the previous chapter we looked at the best way to do this: by testing out those thoughts in real life. But there's a range of other tried-and-tested techniques that you can use in tandem with the behavioural tests and that will make those tests even more effective.

REMEMBER: THOUGHTS ARE NOT FACTS

In Chapter 3 we discovered that in a typical day we experience around 4,000 thoughts. Our head is full of this kind of mental chatter and most of it is utterly inconsequential. The trouble is, we tend to assume our thoughts are much more important than they usually are.

But just because we think something is the case doesn't make it true. We might *think* that our neighbour doesn't like us; we might *think* that we're less intelligent than our work colleagues; we might *think* that things are bound to turn out badly. But it's entirely possible – perhaps even very likely! – that we're mistaken.

How many times have you worried about something only to find out eventually that your anxiety was unjustified? How often have your thoughts led you on a wild goose chase? How many times have you realised that you'd simply been looking at things in the wrong way?

When you experience an anxious thought, remind yourself of these times in your life when your fears proved misplaced. They are testimony to the unreliability of so many of our anxious thoughts.

Our thoughts drift into our mind from who knows where – like flotsam carried by the waves. They come and they go. And most of the time they are no more significant than that flotsam. Remember: *thoughts are not facts!*

THINK OF ALTERNATIVE EXPLANATIONS

If we're prone to anxiety, we can find ourselves giving our anxious thoughts much more credence than they deserve. Francis Bacon, the seventeenth-century scientist and philosopher, wrote:

> *The human understanding when it has once adopted an opinion … draws all things else to support and agree with it. And though there be a greater number and weight of instances to be found on the other side, yet these it either neglects and despises, or else by some distinction sets aside and rejects. (The New Organon, 1620)*

What this means is that two things tend to happen:

★ We notice the things that seem to confirm our anxiety and fail to pick up on those that don't. Psychologists call this phenomenon the *belief confirmation bias*.

★ Because we assume our anxious thoughts are true, we don't consider alternative explanations for events.

This is not to say, of course, that *all* our anxious thoughts are necessarily wrong. Naturally there are occasions when it's right to be worried or fearful. But we can't take our thoughts on trust. We must test them out. Only then will we know whether they really are accurate.

One excellent way of testing our thoughts is to think of alternative explanations for events. A thought, after all, is simply an interpretation of the world. And sometimes anxious thoughts are just the first that come to mind. (If we're often anxious, they may be a bit of reflex.) But other interpretations are always possible – and indeed these alternative viewpoints may well be closer to the truth.

Imagine, for example, that we are at work one day when we pass a colleague in the corridor. 'Hi!' we say with a cheery smile. But our colleague doesn't meet our eye. Instead she mutters 'hello' and walks on.

Why is she being so unfriendly? we think. *What have I done to offend her? Did I mess up something? Doesn't she like me?*

Interpreting other people's behaviour is always tricky because we can never really know what they're thinking. Simply going with our initial negative interpretation is never a good idea. There are many other potential explanations for why our colleague hasn't been as friendly as we would have wished (or indeed for anything else).

She may have been feeling unwell. Or was lost in thought. Perhaps she simply isn't very good at social interactions. Maybe she actually was in a bad mood, but one that had absolutely nothing to do with us – she could have just had an argument with her partner or her boss, for example.

Always try to consider whether there are alternative explanations for the event that has triggered your anxious thoughts. The more you do so, the more natural it will become. To help you get the hang of it, think of a time recently when you felt anxious. What thoughts did you have? And what alternative explanations can you think of? Take a few moments now to jot down your ideas.

Anxious thought:
Alternative explanations:

WEIGH UP THE EVIDENCE FOR YOUR THOUGHTS

The belief confirmation bias means that once we start to believe our anxious thoughts we tend to notice all the evidence that seems to confirm our view and none that doesn't. This is a tendency we need to challenge.

So before you decide that an anxious thought is true, *weigh up the evidence*. You should consider both the evidence that supports the thought *and* the evidence that doesn't.

> *By acknowledging both sides of the argument,*
> *you get a much more balanced perspective.*

Once you do this, you'll generally discover that your first anxious reaction to a situation isn't completely correct. By acknowledging both sides of the argument, you get a much more balanced perspective. And that balanced perspective will give you a far better chance of interpreting your experience accurately. Your anxiety will recede and calmness will grow. What had seemed so worrying just a short time before will suddenly feel much less of a concern.

Let's have a go with the example of the apparently unfriendly colleague. What's the evidence for deciding that she doesn't like us?

It's not as plentiful as we might assume. In fact, it consists solely of the fact that she hasn't greeted us with as much enthusiasm as we expected.

How about the evidence *against* our anxious thought? Well, for a start there's the fact that our colleague has always been very friendly towards us in the past. In fact, come to think of it, she was suggesting a coffee together only the other day – and we had a perfectly nice email from her yesterday morning. We can't think of any reason why she should have changed her attitude towards us – and especially not in the last 24 hours. We know her well enough to be confident that if there were a problem, she'd tell us directly rather than sulking. Moreover, her team has been exceptionally busy over the last couple of weeks, all while being a person short due to illness. If our colleague is preoccupied with her own problems, she has every reason to be.

Spend a few minutes now thinking about the evidence for and against your anxious thoughts. Writing it down is best: you could use a grid like the one below. Take as much time as you need – try to really think through all the possibilities.

Anxious thought:	
Evidence for	Evidence against

Once you've done this for your anxious thought, try doing the same thing for one or more of the alternative explanations you brainstormed earlier.

WRITE ABOUT YOUR WORRIES AND FEARS

Psychologists have discovered that writing down negative thoughts is a wonderfully effective way of overcoming them. This very simple technique is known as *expressive writing*, and here's how you do it.

For around 20 minutes, three or four times a week, jot down your worries. Don't analyse or reflect upon your concerns.

Don't judge your thoughts (and definitely don't judge *yourself*). Try not to explain your worries. Simply write them down. All you're after here is a simple description of your thoughts and feelings – the sort of thing another person could read in order to understand exactly how you've been feeling.

Why does expressive writing work? Well, it helps us to process our thoughts and move on – rather than having them endlessly looping through our brain. It's as if we were physically getting those worries out of our head and on to paper.

Here's an extract from a piece of expressive writing completed by Emma, a 20-year-old student. Emma finds speaking in public very stressful. She was recently asked to give a presentation to her seminar group.

> *Couldn't sleep last night. Full of worries about next week's presentation. I kept thinking, 'What am I doing on this course? I'm going to make a fool of myself. I can't cope. How can I get out of doing the presentation?' These thoughts felt horrible. Lying in bed, I felt stupid and embarrassed. An image flashed into my mind of standing there in class, lost for words. I looked totally bewildered, inept, panic-stricken. Any minute now, I thought, they're going to start laughing at me. I imagined the tutor asking me to see her after the seminar. The worst thought I had was that everything was unravelling: I'd get such a low mark for my presentation that I'd fail the course – and then what would I do? This made me feel really tearful.*

In fact, Emma's presentation turned out to be a far more positive experience than she had anticipated – a success that she attributed in part to her expressive writing:

> *I definitely feel much happier after my writing sessions. It's like I'm taking control and clearing all those nagging worries out of my head. I get some distance, some perspective, some space.*

Writing down my worries allows me to see that they are just thoughts. In my mind, they can seem almost overwhelming, but on paper they look silly and puny.

Schedule some time for your own expressive writing. Relocate your worries from your head and on to the paper. You'll feel so much calmer when you do.

THINK THROUGH YOUR COPING STRATEGIES

Like Emma's night-time worries about public speaking, our anxiety can sometimes seem overwhelming. During our bleakest moments, we feel sure that everything will turn out badly, no matter what we do. We assume that we're powerless in the face of disaster.

Of course, as Emma discovered, the reality usually proves far less scary than we think it's going to be. But imagine that the worst does happen: what could you do then? How might you rescue the situation? What strategies could you use to cope?

> *If you're worried about an upcoming situation, it's worth taking a little time to prepare.*

If you're worried about an upcoming situation, it's worth taking a little time to prepare ahead like this. Write down the outcome you fear and then brainstorm ways to manage the problem.

Emma, for example, worried that she'd be so nervous during her presentation she would forget what she was intending to say. Her mind would go blank; her audience would laugh at her; the presentation would grind to an anguished halt.

Here are some ideas she came up with when she tried this exercise:

★ Make sure I have a few notes within easy reach.

★ Have a joke prepared just in case I dry up.

★ Keep a bottle of water handy – if I'm struggling, I can take a sip and get myself together.

Emma also decided that she'd seek expert advice for her public speaking anxiety. She bought a book on the topic and signed up for a course running at her university. Even before she'd attended the course she felt much happier: 'I was proud of myself for taking action.'

None of us can hope to go through our lives without experiencing another anxious thought. And actually, as we saw in Chapter 1, it wouldn't be a great idea if we did: anxiety can sometimes be a life-saver. Anxiety is normal, natural and necessary.

The problem for many of us, of course, is that the useful kind of anxiety is overshadowed by the negative type: the type that's exaggerated, unrealistic and unjustified. That's the sort of anxiety we most definitely can live without, and that we can learn to overcome.

The secret is not to stop anxious thoughts occurring: that's impossible. Instead, and using the techniques presented in this chapter and the previous one, we can change the way we react to these thoughts.

Rather than simply taking them on trust, we can remind ourselves that they are only thoughts. We can challenge them – weighing up the evidence and thinking of alternative scenarios. We can distance ourselves from them, so that we're able to stand back and decide whether or not they are truly helpful and accurate. And when we do that, the balance of power shifts: we are no longer at the mercy of our anxiety. At last, we are in control.

CHAPTER 5

Reducing worry

We all know what it feels like to worry: it goes with being human. Experts reckon that around four out of ten people worry every day, with the most common topics being work, health, money and relationships. Worry is also a very common feature of anxiety.

Worrying is all about fixing on a particular part of life and imagining what might go wrong. And whether we're fretting about serious issues (*Is my job at risk in the recession?*) or relatively trivial problems (*What if I can't find anything nice to wear to that wedding next month?*), worrying is no fun at all.

When we worry, we try to second-guess the consequences of whichever negative event happens to be on our mind. If I lose my job, will I manage to get another one in the current economic climate? How will I pay the mortgage? Will I end up losing my house? It's for this reason that psychologists sometimes refer to worrying as 'what if?' thinking.

Let's observe this 'what if?' thinking in action. We'll take a very trivial incident: leaving the house without a coat or umbrella and then noticing dark clouds in the distance. Here's how our thoughts might run if we're prone to worry:

★ *What if it rains?* I'll get soaked through.

★ *What if I get soaked through?* I may catch a cold.

★ *What if I catch a cold?* It may develop into pneumonia.

★ *What if I develop pneumonia?* I'll be off work for weeks.

★ *What if I'm off work for weeks?* My employers will think badly of me.

★ *What if my employers think badly of me?* They might try to get rid of me.

So forgetting our coat has ended up costing us our job! This example might seem over the top, but in fact that's the way worry operates. We spend an awful lot of time worrying about disasters that are very unlikely to occur. Our thoughts are skewed: we focus on the negative. And the more we worry, the worse we expect things to turn out: worry feeds on worry.

ASSESSING YOUR LEVEL OF WORRYING

Do you worry more than you'd like to? There's a pretty good chance that the answer to that question is 'yes' because you're reading this book.

But because a certain amount of worrying is normal, how do we judge whether our worrying is getting out of control? Well, a good starting point is to fill in the Penn State Worry Questionnaire.

Enter the number that describes how typical or characteristic each of the following statements is of you, putting the number next to each one.

1	**2**	**3**	**4**	**5**
Not at all typical		Somewhat typical		Very typical

1 If I don't have enough time to do everything, I don't worry about it. ☐

2 My worries overwhelm me. ☐

3 I don't tend to worry about things. ☐

4 Many situations make me worry. ☐

5 I know I shouldn't worry about things, but I just can't help it. ☐

6 When I'm under pressure, I worry a lot. ☐

7 I am always worrying about something. ☐

8 I find it easy to dismiss worrisome thoughts. ☐

9 As soon as I finish one task, I start to worry about something else. ☐

10 I never worry about anything. ☐

11 When there is nothing more I can do about a concern, I don't worry about it any more. ☐

12 I've been a worrier all my life. ☐

13 I notice that I have been worrying about things. ☐

14 Once I start worrying, I can't stop. ☐

15 I worry all the time. ☐

16 I worry about projects until they are all done. ☐

Source: Reprinted from *Behaviour Research and Therapy*, 28(6), Meyer, T.J., Miller, M.L., Metzger, R.L. and Borkovec, T.D., 'Development and validation of the Penn State Worry Questionnaire', pp. 487–95, © 1990, with permission from Elsevier.

Now add up your scores for each statement. Questions 1, 3, 8, 10 and 11 are reversed scored: if, for example, you put 5, for scoring purposes the item is counted as one.

Scores can range from 18 to 80. People with worry problems usually score above 50. But if your total is on the high side, remember that this doesn't prove that you have a problem. To be absolutely sure, you'd need to discuss your situation with a qualified professional.

KEEP A WORRY DIARY

The first step towards getting on top of your worrying is to notice when you're doing it. To help you, use the following worksheet.

Day of the week	When did you worry? For how long (minutes/ hours)?	Triggers: what were you doing just before you started worrying?
Monday		
Tuesday		
Wednesday		
Thursday		
Friday		
Saturday		
Sunday		

Fill in the diary worksheet at the same time each day. It might seem like a bit of a chore, but it'll take only a few minutes. And the benefits will make it well worth your time.

For a start, the diary will help you find out when during the day you're most likely to worry. It'll show you the kinds of things that tend to prompt your worries. You'll be able to get some distance on your worrying: rather than being caught up in it, you'll start to observe it like a scientist conducting an experiment. And if you stick with your diary while you're putting into practice the techniques in this book, you'll be able to see just how far you've come.

RETHINKING YOUR ATTITUDES TOWARDS WORRY

Would you say that worry is a positive or a negative experience?

In the cold light of day, the answer to that question may seem obvious: worry is definitely negative. But research has shown that many people – and particularly those who tend to worry a lot – believe that worry is actually helpful to them. Here are some typical responses:

★ Worrying helps me to look out for difficulties before they happen.

★ If I worry about a problem it prompts me to do something about it.

★ Worrying means that if something bad happens, it isn't a shock.

★ I have this superstitious feeling that if I worry about something it won't happen.

★ Worrying helps me feel in control.

★ If I didn't worry I'd make more mistakes.

Actually, worrying a lot isn't a very good way to achieve any of these positives. (As we've already discovered in this book, thinking something may be true is absolutely no guarantee that it is!) But if we think that worrying helps us in some way, it stands to reason that we're likely to do much more of it than someone who knows that it is futile. Believing that it keeps us safe gives us licence to worry. In fact, worrying may come to seem like the best way to respond to potential trouble: in other words, it becomes a habit.

That might be fine. We could worry away all day if we thought it was helpful (even though it isn't). But, of course, worrying is an unpleasant experience. It makes us tense and unhappy. Rather than improving our mood, worrying just leaves us feeling worse.

Some people even begin to worry *about* their worry. They fear that they will never be able to stop worrying, that worrying means that they are weak, that it'll make them physically ill, or even that worry will drive them insane. (If you've experienced such concerns, you can relax: these negative views about worry are just as inaccurate as the positive ones we've just been discussing.)

> *All in all, then, worrying is pointless,*
> *unhelpful and unpleasant.*

All in all, then, worrying is pointless, unhelpful and unpleasant. So there are plenty of good reasons to do less of it! A good place to start tackling worry is to review your beliefs about it. What purpose do you believe it serves? Do you feel it might sometimes be beneficial? How do you think it might help you?

If you find that you're harbouring positive thoughts about worry, you need to challenge those assumptions. To do this, think back to a recent bout of worry. When you reflect on your experience, did the advantages you thought you might get from worrying materialise? Did worrying really help? Did it make you feel better, or help you tackle whatever problem was on your mind? Was it worth all that time and effort? Could there be better ways of dealing with your fears than worrying about them?

You'll almost certainly come to the conclusion that you'd have been better off not worrying at all. You'll see that your positive beliefs about worry are unjustified. And that will help you break free from them.

USE WORRY PERIODS

One of the particularly horrible things about worry is the way that it can come to dominate our thoughts. No matter where we are or what we're doing – at times when we know we *should* be absorbed in the present moment – our mind is elsewhere, rehashing the same nagging worries.

If worry is taking up more of your time and mental energy than you'd like, you can turn that around by using the technique psychologists call 'worry periods'. Set aside 15 minutes each day and save all your worrying for then. Choose somewhere private, set the alarm on your mobile phone and deliberately give yourself up to your worries. Don't sit on the sofa or lie on your bed: sit at a table on an upright chair. If this feels uncomfortable, so much the better! You don't want worrying to be in any way relaxing or pleasurable.

Aim to schedule your worry period for the same time every day – that'll help it become a habit. Lots of people opt for 6pm: they can deal with whatever worries have accumulated during the day, but it's not too close to bedtime. Your last activity before sleep should be something relaxing, and definitely not worrying.

If you find yourself worrying at other times of the day, stop. Easier said than done, you might object. But there are several tricks you can use to help. Try writing down what's on your mind and telling yourself that you'll think it through later. You might prefer to distract yourself with some kind of activity. Some people find it effective to clap their hands and say 'not now' when they notice that they're worrying. Others use mindfulness techniques to let their anxious thoughts pass by. They watch the worry come into their mind, acknowledge it, but don't let it distract them. They stay as calm as they can, focus on what they're doing and not what they're thinking, and watch the waves of their worries recede into the distance. (You'll find more about mindfulness in Chapter 10.) Which strategies do you think might work best for you?

Postponing worry like this may seem hard at first, but you'll soon get used to it. Remember: you're not imposing a 'no worry' rule. You'll have plenty of opportunity to mull over what's bugging you. You're just setting a few limits, drawing a line between worrying and the rest of your day.

You'll find that this is a great way of limiting your worrying. But that isn't all: many people discover that they can gradually cut the duration of their worry periods, from 15 minutes to 10 and from 10 to 5. Some people even notice that they can manage quite happily without them. They have broken the habit of worrying.

WORK OUT WHEN YOU'RE MOST VULNERABLE TO WORRY – AND BE PREPARED!

There's usually a pattern when it comes to worrying. We're more likely to worry at certain times of the day or night than at others. We're more vulnerable when we find ourselves in particular situations.

Now the fact that there is a pattern is a big help when we're trying to reduce our worrying. Because if we can identify those problematic times and situations, we can prepare for them. Many people find that they worry most first thing in the morning and last thing at night, probably because those are the times when they're not busy doing something else.

Have a look at your worry diary. Are you more likely to worry at certain times of the day or night? Can you identify particular situations that trigger your worrying? What are you doing, or feeling, or thinking when worry begins?

Let's imagine you notice that you're most prone to worry first thing in the morning, or at other times when you find yourself at a loose end. How can you prevent those negative thoughts from creeping in?

> *Your job is to deny worry the time and space it needs to grow.*

Well, one very effective strategy is to make sure you're busy doing something absorbing. Worry loves empty time: when we're not engaged by some activity, our mind is at the mercy of our most negative thoughts. So your job is to deny worry the time and space it needs to grow.

Exactly which kind of activity you opt for is entirely your choice. Everyone will have their own preferences. But experts know that certain types of activity are especially effective worry deterrents.

Being physically active

Have you ever noticed what happens when you're playing a sport, swimming or running, singing or playing a musical instrument? Time seems to zip past. We lose ourselves in the moment. And we don't worry – our mind is totally focused on what we're doing. Psychologists call this experience 'flow', and it's a fantastic way of boosting our mood.

Draw up a list of your favourite activities, pastimes and hobbies – the ones that take your mind off your worries. Then make sure you're spending at least a little time every day doing one of them. Put it in your diary: even though it's an appointment with yourself, you're more likely to keep that appointment if you schedule it in. Try to slot in the activity at the times when you're most prone to worry. So rather than lying in bed worrying first thing in the morning, it's far better to get busy with something you find rewarding – going for a run, perhaps, or working in the garden. (For more on flow, see page 91.)

Talking to people

The human mind is astonishingly sophisticated and yet it isn't very good at doing two things at once. This is why being physically active is such an effective barrier against negative thoughts – and why talking to other people is also a great way to shut out worry.

In fact, research suggests that probably the biggest single contributor to happiness is the quality of our relationships with friends and/or family. So when you feel worry creeping up on you, make contact with someone – chances are, all it will take is a phone call, or even just a few steps into the next room.

Focusing your thoughts on the positive

There are times, of course, when we can't simply go out for a run or call up a friend for a chat. If we're soaking in the bath, or stuck in a meeting at work, or lying in bed at night, we're probably going to need a different strategy to combat worry. These are the times to use one of the following techniques.

★ *Think of a positive memory*. Close your eyes and focus on a time when you were truly happy. Try to recall as many details as you can. Who was there? What were they wearing? What was the weather like? How did you feel? What did you all do or say? What made the experience so special?

★ *Celebrate your positive qualities.* Again, close your eyes and this time bring to mind some achievement, skill or personal characteristic that gives you pride. If you're feeling very anxious or low, this might seem tricky. But don't give up: all you need is one thing that makes you feel good about yourself. Perhaps you're thoughtful or kind, brave or hard-working; maybe you're a talented musician or cook; perhaps you did very well in an exam, or trained for a charity run, or helped someone out. Repeat to yourself: 'I am good at …' Or 'I was proud of myself when …'

★ *Ask yourself: what's the best thing that could happen?* Worry is a negative state of mind; it's all about what might go wrong. So let's switch it around. Choose a situation or problem that's been worrying you and imagine: what is the best thing that could happen?

Practising a relaxation exercise

It's very difficult to worry when we're genuinely relaxed – indeed, overcoming negative thoughts and feelings is one of the main goals of techniques such as meditation or yoga. Pick one or more of the relaxation exercises discussed in Chapter 10 and make them a regular feature of your day, ideally at a time when you're most susceptible to worry.

ACCEPT UNCERTAINTY

How do you feel about uncertainty? Does it excite you? Do you enjoy the sensation of not knowing for sure what's going to happen? Or, given the choice, would you opt for certainty all the way?

If you're not keen on uncertainty, welcome to the club: most of us feel that way. We like to know what's in store for us. But, as you'll have noticed, life often won't play ball. We might prefer certainty, but what we *get* is often exactly the reverse.

Now, the fact that we can't know for sure what's going to happen next in our lives opens the door to worry. In fact, psychologists have noticed that people who worry a lot tend to be especially, and continually, unsettled by uncertainty.

Worriers often assume that uncertainty is inherently bad. How, they might think, can we make a decision if we can't be sure how things will turn out? How can we get on with our life when we don't know what's around the corner – and especially when what's around that corner is bound to be awful? How can we prevent the worst happening if we don't know when and in what way it will happen?

> *We have to make our peace with uncertainty.*

We have to make our peace with uncertainty. We have to accept that no action is 100 per cent risk-free. And that no matter how much we try, we can't totally control events. Attempting to do so is a guaranteed route to exhaustion, stress and disappointment. Besides, would constant certainty be such a great thing? Wouldn't life become stale and boring? Wouldn't we end up yearning for the unexpected?

Our life, just like everyone else's, will include highs and lows. No matter how much we worry, we can't know what's in store for us. And we can't prevent problems happening just by worrying about them. So instead of dwelling on possible – though unlikely – disasters in an uncertain future, it's far better to focus on the present. And especially to concentrate on and celebrate the positive things in our lives right now.

Have a think about your worries. Does uncertainty play a role? Does your anxiety stem in part from the feeling that you don't know how things will turn out? Does that feeling result in you fearing the worst? Does not knowing frighten you, or make you stressed?

Here's an exercise that's designed to develop our tolerance for uncertainty. The idea is simple: we go looking for uncertainty and we see what happens. The tasks can be as small as you like: cooking something you've never tried before, perhaps, or reading a book you wouldn't normally think of picking up. You could change your daily routine, or start saying 'yes' when you'd generally say 'no'. You might try chatting to someone new, or allowing yourself to act on impulse. And afterwards, ask yourself: did things turn out as badly as you feared, or much better than you had ever expected?

The techniques we've presented in this chapter have all been proven to help people overcome their problems with worry. They have worked for thousands of individuals and they will work for you, too. All that's required is a little perseverance. The reward is definitely worth it.

But these aren't the only strategies you can use. What does worry grow from and focus on? Problems – or rather situations that we perceive as potential problems. We may be able to solve many of those problems. And if we can, those worries will vanish. So that's where we turn in the following chapter: mastering worry by developing our problem-solving skills.

CHAPTER 6

Problem solving

At the core of most worry lies a potential problem. How will I manage at that day-long course when I don't know any of the other people attending? How can I tell my child's teacher that I'm unhappy about what happened at school last week? What should I cook for our guests next weekend? How will I cope with those medical tests? How on earth am I going to be able to pay for that holiday?

With some worries, we're in the realm of the uncertain: problems we fear may crop up some time in the future. There's often nothing we can do right now about these potential problems, so the best thing is to let them go.

But there are some problems – such as the ones listed above – that we can definitely do something about. And if we can find a satisfactory solution to these problems, our worries are likely to disappear, too. So that's what we're going to focus on in this chapter: improving our problem-solving skills. Or in other words, learning how to swap exhausting, stressful, unproductive worry for decisive, effective and morale-raising action.

HOW DO YOU RATE YOUR PROBLEM-SOLVING SKILLS?

How do you generally react to problems? Are you confident in your ability to sort them out successfully? Do you act quickly to deal with the issue? Do you find it pretty easy to think up and implement possible solutions?

Or do you tend to assume that a problem is likely to lead to disaster? Does it seem as though there's nothing you can do? Or that if you were to try tackling the problem, it would be bound to go horribly wrong?

The way in which you respond to problems may well depend on the kind of issue you're facing. You might be fine with practical problems, but feel all at sea when it comes to dealing with other people. Perhaps you're particularly flummoxed by money matters, or stressed out by worries about your loved ones, or anxious about your health.

Of course, if we believe we're facing a problem we can't resolve, it's likely to prey on our mind. We'll probably feel stressed and anxious and miserable. However, if we're confident that we can sort out a problem, it's unlikely to worry us. We don't usually lie awake fretting about an issue that we know we can cope with. Sure, we might prefer that the problem hadn't arisen, and we might not be overjoyed about the effort or expense it generates, but we won't spend long worrying about it.

And that's where we want to get to. We want to feel confident in our ability to tackle the widest range of problems. When issues arise, we want to be able to say to ourselves: *I can handle this*. And mean it.

> *The good news is that problem solving is a skill that we can all learn.*

The good news is that problem solving is a skill that we can all learn. It is not, as they say, rocket science! Instead it boils down to following a few logical steps. But before we get to those practical steps, it's worth spending a little time thinking about your attitude to problems.

Which are the problems that make you worry? Do you doubt whether you can handle these issues? What are the negative thoughts that come to mind when you think about your ability to deal with problems? If you're aware of these thoughts, you can spot them when they arise – you can gain distance and perspective – and so be much better placed to see that they are simply thoughts and not reality.

As you sift through your negative thoughts, bear in mind that you are *already* an experienced and accomplished problem solver. Seem unlikely? But think through an average day: over and over again you're making decisions and overcoming difficulties. Whether we're deciding what to cook for supper, handling issues at work, looking after our children, or discussing issues with our partner, we are all continually shaping events into something closer to how we'd like them. We are, in other words, solving problems.

The trick is to recognise this, sharpen our skills (we can all benefit from that) and then apply those skills to the problems that trigger our worry.

HOW TO BOOST YOUR PROBLEM-SOLVING SKILLS

Learning to notice your negative thoughts will be a big help. But even better is to improve your problem-solving skills and to see the positive results. You'll realise – perhaps to your surprise – that you can cope. That you don't simply have to hope things will turn out okay. That you can take action and influence events. And when that happens, you'll find that you're worrying much less and feeling far calmer.

In Chapter 5 we introduced the idea of using worry periods: you save up all your worries for a daily 15-minute time slot. After a while, you'll almost certainly find that you don't need these worry periods any longer. You can then use that time to problem solve.

Step 1: Decide whether the problem can be solved

There are, of course, some problems that can't be solved. For example, scientists expect the earth to be swallowed by the dying sun in several billion years' time. As things currently stand this is a problem without a solution. So if we're worrying about it, and we want to worry less, we're going to have to use one of the other strategies in this book. We can, for instance, learn to get some distance from our negative thoughts; to boost our positive thoughts; to relax; or to savour the moment.

Some problems can't be solved by us. We might be very concerned about the global economic situation, but for most of us any remedies lie way beyond our sphere of influence.

And some potential problems can't be – or don't need to be – solved by us right now. There's little point in worrying about how you'd feel if you fell out with your best friend, for example, when you're getting on perfectly well.

So step 1 is to ask yourself whether your problem can be solved, and more specifically whether it can be solved by you right now. Of course, people with a low opinion of their problem-solving skills may wonder whether they can resolve *any* problem. If you tend to think like this, try to put those thoughts aside for a moment. Ask yourself: if I were better at solving problems (and very soon you will be), could I solve this one?

Step 2: Define the problem in as much detail as possible

Have you ever attempted to complete a jigsaw without looking at the picture on the box? We don't recommend it.

Similarly, it's much easier to deal with a problem when we have a clear sense of what that problem involves. What's really on our mind? What's troubling us? Make sure you sit down with a pen and paper – writing things down helps us to concentrate and to gain perspective on our thoughts.

Remember Emma from Chapter 4? Emma's a student who finds the thought of speaking in public very stressful. Here's how she defined her problem:

What's the problem? I have to give a presentation to our seminar group on a topic of my choice in a month's time. There'll be about 25 people there, including my tutor and lots of my friends. But I've never spoken in front of a large group before. The thought fills me with dread. And my anxiety is paralysing me: I can't start work on the presentation. I can't even decide what the presentation is going to be about. So I guess my problem is that I have to give this talk and I don't know how on earth I'm going to manage to get through it. I worry that I might be too anxious to do it and that I might be asked to leave the group.

Step 3: Think of possible solutions

Once you've clearly identified the problem, it's time to start thinking of solutions – as many as you can. Again, do this sitting down at a table or desk, with a pen and paper: it'll help you focus on the task.

That blank sheet of paper can seem very intimidating. But the first idea is often the hardest. Write down the first thing that comes to mind, no matter how silly it might seem. When you're generating ideas, it's best not to judge them – for the moment all that matters is that you get them down on paper.

If you're struggling to come up with ideas, try to remember what's worked for you in the past. Imagine what you'd tell someone who came to you with the same problem, or what a person you admire might do. But best of all, ask someone you trust for advice – even when you have a few ideas of your own.

Here are some of the possible solutions that Emma came up with:

★ *Phone in sick on the day of the presentation.*

★ *Explain to my tutor how I feel and ask whether I can skip the presentation.*

★ *Explain to my tutor how I feel so that she can bear that in mind when she marks the presentation.*

★ *Stop putting it off and instead sit down and write a really good presentation so that I can feel as confident as possible when I talk to the group.*

★ *Talk to my parents and friends to see whether they have any tips on how to speak in public.*

★ *Look on the internet and in the library for advice on public speaking. See whether I can find a course on public speaking. Use the ideas I find to help me overcome my anxiety.*

Step 4: Weigh up the pros and cons of your potential solutions

By this stage in the process, you've decided whether you have a problem you can do something about right now, you've clarified the problem and you've brainstormed possible ways to tackle it. Now it's time to evaluate those solutions, to weigh up their advantages and disadvantages.

Possible solution:	
Advantages	Disadvantages

Here's an excerpt from the notes Emma made when she did this exercise:

Possible solution: *phone in sick on the day of the presentation*	
Advantages	Disadvantages
I don't have to give the presentation	Actually, I might well have to do it another day. If not, I'd probably get marked down
	I'll have to lie
	I'll feel ashamed and cowardly
	Next time I'm asked to do something similar I'll have the same problem

▶

Possible solution: *explain to my tutor how I feel and ask whether I can skip the presentation*

Advantages	Disadvantages
I might not have to give the presentation	She might tell me I have to do it
	She might think badly of me for asking
	It would be embarrassing
	Again, won't help me next time I have to do something like this

Possible solution: *explain to my tutor how I feel so that she can bear that in mind when she marks the presentation*

Advantages	Disadvantages
If I perform badly because of nerves, I may not lose marks	I'll still have to do the presentation
I do the presentation: I face up to the task	I'll probably still worry about it
I'll probably feel pleased with myself for not ducking the presentation	I'll look weak and my tutor might think badly of me
	I'll find it embarrassing to talk to my tutor about my anxiety
	I'll still feel anxious next time I have to give some kind of speech

Possible solution: *stop putting it off and instead sit down and write a really good presentation so that I can feel as confident as possible when I talk to the group*

Advantages	Disadvantages
I won't be wasting any more time	I'm not sure this is a complete solution; I think there's probably more I can do

I'll have the presentation written	
I'll probably feel less nervous	

Possible solution: *talk to my parents and friends to see whether they have any tips on how to speak in public*

Advantages	Disadvantages
I know my mum does a lot of public speaking for work so she may well have some good ideas	What if the people I ask can't help?
I'll probably learn a lot	I might find it embarrassing. Will people think less of me?
If it's a helpful exercise, I'll be less nervous when I give the presentation	
I'll be less anxious in the future	

Possible solution: *look on the internet and in the library for advice on public speaking. See whether I can find a course on public speaking. Use the ideas I find to help me overcome my anxiety*

Advantages	Disadvantages
I know lots of people don't like public speaking; there's bound to be information out there. Actually, I think I remember seeing that the university runs a course	May be time-consuming
Will probably help me with the presentation	May not help
Will also help me deal with similar stuff in the future	
I'll feel really pleased and proud of myself for acknowledging the problem and taking action	

Step 5: Choose a solution, decide how you're going to carry it out, and go for it!

Once you've weighed up the advantages and disadvantages of your potential solutions, you can move on to the next step of the process: selecting the option that seems most promising.

> *Go for the solution that seems best and if it doesn't work out you can try another.*

Making a decision may seem daunting. But you'll find that having your list of pros and cons in front of you will help enormously. And, as we'll see in a moment, all you're going to do is *try* a solution. If you later come to the conclusion that a different option might have been better, that's fine: you can move on to that. So remember that you're not tied to this decision for ever: go for the solution that seems best and if it doesn't work out you can try another. It's all part of the problem-solving process.

When you make your choice, have a think about how exactly you're going to put your solution into practice. What are the tasks you'll need to carry out? In what order would it be best to tackle them? Which should you start with? Can you think of any problems you might run into? What could you do to deal with them? And could you combine this strategy with any of the others on your list?

Here's what Emma did:

> *I decided to focus on the last option: looking for information that would help me cope with my anxiety about public speaking and then, of course, actually using that information! But I did also sit down and start work on the presentation. I can't say I'd been looking forward to it. But I didn't want to put it off to the last*

minute. I knew that wouldn't help when I eventually had to stand up in front of the group.

I started off by making a list of possible sources of material, and then I tried to do one thing every couple of days. For example, one day I spent looking at self-help books on the internet; another day I checked out the local bookshop; and then I tracked down the course on public speaking that I remembered seeing advertised at university, and enrolled on it. Once I'd bought a relevant book, I set myself a target of reading a certain number of pages a day. When it came to actually using the techniques I came across, I was worried that I might find it all a bit overwhelming, or maybe a bit boring. So again I set myself targets: trying one new technique a day. I'm one of those people who finds it much easier to cope if I have a list and a schedule. I also gave my mum a ring. We had a brilliant talk and she gave me some really useful advice.

Step 6: Review how you got on

After you've tried your solution, sit down again with your pen and paper and review how you got on. Did things go well? Did you solve your problem?

If things didn't turn out quite as successfully as you had hoped, that's no big deal. Simply look through your list of solutions and see whether there's another strategy that might work. And if there isn't, don't worry: go back to step 1 of the process and rethink the possibilities. You'll get there in the end, for sure.

Here's Emma again:

The presentation went so much better than I would ever have believed. I was nervous, but I don't think it showed. I managed to get over the points I wanted to make, and people seemed very interested. We had a great discussion afterwards and I was really pleased with the mark I got from my tutor. More than that, I feel as if I've made a breakthrough. I'm not saying I'll be jumping for joy the next time I have to do something similar. But I won't worry. I'll know that I can do it.

Problem solving is all about taking a logical approach to life's hassles and difficulties. Because it's logical, there's no mystery. We can all learn how to do it. And when we do, we take a huge, liberating, confidence-boosting leap forward. Instead of focusing on the negative, we open up to the positive and constructive steps we can take to make our life better. Rather than going round in circles, we start moving forwards. And that feels *so* good.

CHAPTER 7

Tackling negative images

I see myself looking foolish and awkward – as if I'd rather be anywhere else in the world right now. I'm shrinking away from the people I'm with. I'm stumbling over my words, sounding like someone who has only just started learning English. I know I'm making no sense at all. My face is absurd and ugly – pasty cheeks, sweat dripping from my forehead, skin blotchy with spots. And my hair looks like I've cut it myself.

As a species, we human beings pride ourselves on our thinking skills. Armed with our amazingly complex languages, we can logically analyse, plan, discuss and problem solve. The rest of the animal world doesn't stand a chance …

But of course, much of what goes on in our heads isn't like this at all. We don't always think logically – in fact, much of the time we're doing nothing of the sort. And our mind isn't simply busy with verbal thoughts, it is also full of images: pictures of ourselves and the world around us, both real and fictitious.

Though people tend not to talk about them, images can play a powerful role in emotions, and perhaps particularly in anxiety. Without warning, we suddenly see ourselves in the situations we fear: sitting with our boss while he explains his serious concerns about our performance; answering the phone that rings with bad news of our loved ones; watching the colour drain from our face as the plane lurches and dips, the warning lights flash on and the cabin staff try to mask their obvious panic; or, as in the quotation at the beginning of this chapter, making a fool of ourselves in a social situation.

These vivid images can be extremely upsetting, dominating our thoughts and sending us into a tailspin of anxiety. So it's really important that we learn to combat them. And we can, in three ways:

★ Letting go of our negative images.

★ Reworking them.

★ Replacing them with positive images.

Which one of these options you choose is up to you. Give each of them a try and see what works best.

LETTING GO OF YOUR NEGATIVE IMAGES

Earlier we made the point that *thoughts are not facts*. Actually, it's one of the most important lessons we'd like readers to take away from this book, because it'll help you get crucial distance from the negative thoughts that fuel anxiety.

It's the same with negative images. Somehow we have to break their spell. We must deprive them of their power over us. We need to recognise that they are only images. Like thoughts, we have to understand that just because they appear in our mind does not mean they are true.

One great way of doing this is to develop what's known as a mindful attitude to the images. You'll find a lot more information about mindfulness, along with several calming practical exercises, in Chapter 10. But in essence what we want you to practise is letting these images go.

When you find that a negative image has appeared in your mind, don't fight it. Don't try to pretend that it hasn't occurred. Instead, acknowledge its presence. Say to yourself: 'Ah, there's that image again of …' And then let it pass – as it surely will, and far quicker if you don't engage with it.

To give you a sense of what we're aiming for here, imagine that you're lying in a field on a warm summer's day. You are engrossed in a book – it's something you've been looking forward to reading for months and finally you have the time. Every so often, and for just a few seconds, you lift your gaze from your book. And when you do this you occasionally notice a plane far off in the sky: so far away, in fact, that it is little more than a speck. Idly, you watch the plane disappear and then return to your book.

We want you to treat your negative images as you would that plane. You see it, but you don't waste time thinking about it. It's not important. Instead, your focus stays on what you're doing. And very soon the image fades into the distance.

REWORKING YOUR NEGATIVE IMAGES

Unpleasant images can be enormously powerful – so powerful, in fact, that it may never occur to us that they are simply mental pictures. And pictures can always be altered, as we're going to show you now.

This is an exercise you can do at any point during the day. You don't have to wait for a negative image to appear. In fact, it's best to do it as preparation for those moments.

The exercise will take only a few minutes of your time, though it's best to do it several times each day. Like most things, the more often you practise, the better you'll get. The better you get, the fewer negative images you'll experience and the less you'll be distressed by any that do occur.

Though it's only for a very short time, you'll want to really focus on the images. Try to immerse yourself in the scene, and not only what you see but also what you feel, smell or hear. To help you do this, try to find somewhere quiet where you won't be disturbed. It's a good idea to close your eyes, too – that will make it easier to shut out the world around you and concentrate on the task at hand.

Before you set about reworking your negative images, though, you have to identify them. So step one is to sit down with pen and paper and make a list of the upsetting images you've experienced lately. Sometimes they're based on frightening events that have happened to us in the past – or that we've heard about or seen happening to other people. Sometimes they're inspired by 'near misses': occasions when we believe we narrowly avoided disaster. And often they seem just to appear from nowhere and with no reason. Which negative images have been troubling you? What experiences might they have their roots in?

> *From now on, you are in charge and not some puny imaginary picture!*

Once you have your list of negative images, choose one to work on first. What you're going to do is to gain control over this image. It's time to turn the tables – from now on, you are in charge and not some puny imaginary picture!

How do you do this? It's simple: you change the image. You play about with it. You learn that you can do anything you like with it.

One of the characteristics of anxious images is that we tend to see ourselves from the perspective of another person. We are passive. We are trapped in the scene. It's as if the image were a photograph – a photograph that shows us looking silly or in some kind of danger.

But although it doesn't feel like it, we took that photo, we have the negative or digital file, and we can alter it however we choose. Here are three techniques for you to try.

Imagine that the image is a picture on TV

What could you do? Well, what about altering the colour – maybe even turning it into black and white? You could lower the volume (remember that you can change anything about the image, not just what you see). You might try another channel: you're bound to be able to find something more enjoyable to look at. Or you could even switch off the set completely.

Update the image

There are two main ways to do this. The first is to remove the negative features of the scene. So if your image shows you struggling to chat to new people, you can scrub out the sweat on your brow, the nervous expression on your face, the awkward pause while you try desperately to think of something interesting to say. If it helps, you could pretend that you're working with a photo-editing program on your computer – you highlight an unwanted bit of the image with your mouse, click Delete and it vanishes instantly.

The other strategy is to make the image as positive as you possibly can. No longer do you see yourself paralysed by fear as the plane's captain announces that an engine has failed. Instead, your new image shows you chatting happily to the friendly passenger in the next seat, while a smiling flight attendant pours your favourite drink and the aircraft sails smoothly through the cloudless sky.

Why not try running this positive image on? Imagine that, having paused the movie to focus on this particular moment, you're now pressing Play. So, for example, you watch as the flight proceeds without a hitch, touching down right on time at your destination, where – to your delight – a loved one has unexpectedly come to meet you.

Spend a few sessions practising with these updated images. You want them to become totally familiar. That way, if the upsetting version makes a reappearance, you'll be ready for it.

Use humour

Children tend to receive an awful lot of advice. And perhaps because there is so much of it, lots of this advice never registers. The child takes absolutely no notice and before long the advice is totally forgotten. Occasionally, though, something sticks and for us it was the recommendation that when we are afraid of someone we can get the better of our anxiety by … imagining them naked.

This is an approach that you can also bring to your negative images: you undermine them with the aid of humour. Perhaps you're worried about a job interview and keep imagining yourself being grilled by a panel of glum and unforgiving inter-viewers. You could use the naked trick. Alternatively, you might visualise, say, a herd of cows ambling through the office. Or a water pipe bursting above the panel's heads.

It doesn't matter what you choose, as long as it makes you smile. Because when you do, the anxious image that once made you feel so bad will suddenly seem ridiculous. And its power over you will be gone.

A word about coping with nightmares

When we're very anxious, it would be lovely to think that at the end of the day we can at least close our eyes and enjoy eight hours of deep, relaxing, stress-free sleep. Unfortunately, it's not always that simple. For a start, our worries may mean that we struggle to fall asleep, or to stay asleep. (If you're struggling with insomnia, be sure to read Chapter 11.) And when we do sleep, anxious images can intrude in the form of vivid nightmares.

Like our dreams, nightmares are usually highly visual. Though we might find it difficult to recall many of our happy dreams, with nightmares we often have a different problem: we remember them only too well. Certainly, the unpleasant emotions they trigger – typically fear and anxiety but sometimes anger, grief or sadness – can stick around long after we've woken up.

If you're struggling with nightmares, the good news is that a very effective treatment has been developed specifically to help people cope. That treatment is called *imagery rehearsal* and it's similar to some of the techniques we've just described for reworking your negative images.

Essentially, you need to retell the story of your nightmare. But this time you're in control. That means you can change the story any way you like. Perhaps you might remove a particularly unpleasant event, or delete a threatening person: imagine how satisfying *that* will feel! Maybe you could introduce a friendly face – someone you'd much rather see in your dreams. And why not add in a happy ending?

Spend a few minutes every day running through this new version in your mind. Gradually, you'll find that the events of your nightmare become much less disturbing. And when that happens, other positive changes will follow. You'll experience fewer nightmares, and if they do happen they'll be far less intense.

It's worth remembering, incidentally, that poor sleep can cause nightmares. A vicious circle can spring up: nightmares interfere with our sleep, which then makes us more susceptible to nightmares. So if you can improve your quality of sleep – and the techniques we describe in Chapter 11 will help you achieve that – you'll also be helping to protect yourself from nightmares.

REPLACING NEGATIVE IMAGES WITH POSITIVE ONES

So far we've discovered how we can prevent negative images from making us feel anxious. But now let's find out how we can boost our mood by using *positive* images.

You can practise the exercises we're about to describe to you at any time, but we think they may be especially useful before you go into the kind of situations that make you anxious. They'll help you to feel calmer, more relaxed and confident. They'll provide you with a template for success.

As we've mentioned previously in this book, focusing on more than one thing at a time is way beyond most of us. Asking someone to think of one happy and one sad event simultaneously is like asking them to cook dinner while painting the ceiling. Something has to give. If you can quickly summon up a positive image, you'll soon find that it's far preferable to the negative image that usually appears in your mind.

> *In positive images we tend to do the*
> *seeing. We are active, not passive.*

Here are three exercises you can practise to generate positive images, either to use in preparation for anxious situations or simply to help you relax. What you'll notice is that when you're experiencing these kinds of mental pictures, you're seeing things from a different perspective – literally. Remember how negative images seem to show us from the perspective of another person? Well, in positive images we tend to do the seeing. We are active, not passive. We look at the world, rather than the world looking at us. We are in control. It's a really significant difference.

Visualise success

Sports psychology has become extremely influential in recent years, with athletes and coaches now understanding that mental preparation can play a huge part in improving performance. As former Olympic champion Dame Kelly Holmes said: 'It's what goes on in your head that counts.'

One of the key techniques used by sportsmen and women is visualisation, which involves deliberately conjuring up mental images of success. Olympic gold medallist Jessica Ennis is certainly a big fan:

> *I use a lot of visualisation. I visualise the whole heptathlon a day before, two days before I compete and also during the event as well. It allows me to go through the perfect motion of what I want to achieve from each event. And it gives me a really positive outlook before I go out and compete.*

If it works for Jessica Ennis, it can work for the rest of us, too! Choose a situation that would normally make you anxious: giving a speech, perhaps. And then imagine that things go as well as they possibly could. For example, you're speaking fluently without once looking at your notes. You feel full of confidence and charm; you know you're carrying it off perfectly. When you look at your audience, you see that they are spell-bound, clearly absorbed in what you have to say. They laugh loudly at all your jokes, and when you've finished they gather round to congratulate you on your speech. You feel flushed with pleasure and pride.

Imagine your own personal life coach

If you're finding things tough, who do you turn to? In an ideal world, who would you *like* to have beside you when you're feeling anxious? Who do you look up to as a role model?

Whoever that person may be – and it could be someone you know well, someone you've read about or seen on TV, someone real or someone fictional – we want you to practise conjuring up their image in your mind.

Try to visualise their face, their posture, their tone of voice. See how kind and caring they are towards you. Notice how they understand just what to say in order to calm your anxiety; how wise their advice is; how adept they are at knowing when all you really need is a loving hug. And how, if you simply learn to call them to mind, they'll be there for you whenever you need them.

Imagine a safe place

Where in the world have you felt relaxed and serene and secure? Close your eyes now and spend a few moments thinking about possible locations – places that spark in you only positive memories and feelings; where you felt your worries fall from you; where you would love to return one day. (In fact, perhaps it's somewhere you've never been, but where you're certain you would be happy and calm.)

Perhaps you'll choose a gorgeous, sun-kissed beach. Or a pretty cottage in the depths of idyllic countryside. Or maybe a remote mountain lodge, with the sun setting and the sound of goats bleating happily in the distance. Whatever you decide on, try to visualise it in as much detail as you can. Imagine the colours, the smell, the sounds, the sensation of the breeze or the sun on your skin.

Take a little time each day to think about this safe place. Really fix it in your imagination. Then you'll be able to call upon it whenever a negative image comes to mind – or indeed the next time you're feeling anxious or unhappy.

Negative images often sneak under the radar. We tend to assume our thoughts are verbal rather than pictorial. But the images in our mind are sometimes powerful drivers of emotion, and research suggests that they can be especially damaging in anxiety.

If you practise using the techniques in this chapter to overcome your negative images, you'll soon feel calmer and more content. Gradually you'll find that those anxious images appear in your mind far less often. And eventually they may disappear altogether.

CHAPTER 8

Switching your focus of attention

Mark is a 51-year-old car mechanic. He thinks of himself as shy, and finds it stressful to deal with customers he doesn't already know.

I tend to keep myself busy with the vehicles and stay away from the office. I prefer to let one of the other guys handle the customers. But that's not always possible. Sometimes I have to take a turn in the office, and customers will also sometimes just come straight up to you while you're working on their car. Then I'm quite nervous. I know I'm not great at dealing with other people. I can't seem to get my words out properly. I feel like I'm blushing red as a beetroot. The customers must think I'm an idiot. The longer I'm with them, the worse I imagine it'll get. So I try to get things over with as quickly as I can, before I embarrass myself even more. I answer their questions briefly and I certainly don't do social chat. But I worry that the customers will think I'm rude.

What's striking about Mark's story is his attitude to those times when he has to deal directly with a customer. He assumes that things will go badly. What he notices are the things that seem to confirm his fears (feeling himself blush, for example, or finding it difficult to make small talk). And so his goal becomes a very simple one: to make the meeting as short as possible.

Mark's experience reminds us that, as we saw earlier, much of our anxiety is in our head. How we feel is a response not to a real-life situation but to a situation that we believe may occur: it's a psychological reaction to imagined future danger. Mark isn't anxious because he's made a fool of himself but because he *thinks* he's going to do so. And we all get it wrong sometimes. We see threat where, in reality, there is none. We exaggerate the danger.

When we do, an interesting thing happens. Like Mark with a customer, we direct our attention to the potentially negative aspects of the situation. We look for signs that our fear is justified and ignore what doesn't fit our script. Our only goal is to avoid disaster.

This is what psychologists call a *negative focus of attention*. And it locks us into our anxiety. It fuels our worries. It feeds our fear.

> *If we can focus on something more positive, our anxiety will ease.*

But if we can switch our attention, if we can focus on something more positive, our anxiety will ease. We'll feel calmer. We'll be able to shrug off our worries and get on with the rest of our day. This chapter will show you how to do it.

CHANGE YOUR GOALS

When Mark feels anxious, his goals reflect his negative focus of attention. For Mark, it's all about damage limitation: his goal is to end the meeting as quickly as possible, before he's embarrassed himself too much. Of course, this kind of mindset only reinforces Mark's preoccupation with the negative aspects of the situation.

Spend a little time now thinking about your own anxiety. What happens to your attention in these situations? What do your thoughts home in on? And what are your goals? What would be a successful outcome for you?

One great way of shifting your focus of attention is to change your goals. Instead of trying simply to avoid disaster, let's switch things around. Let's ask ourselves: what positives can we take from these stressful situations? Here's what Mark came up with when he tried this exercise:

> I decided to try to enjoy the meetings with customers. And to be as friendly and professional as I could. I smiled, made eye contact, asked the customers questions. It didn't come easily at first, but I modelled myself on my boss, who is really good at that sort of thing. Although it shouldn't really surprise me, the more effort I made, the easier it became – and the better I got on with the customers. And one day, as I was standing there chatting to a guy, it suddenly struck me: I'm not anxious! It was an amazing feeling.

Now it's your turn. What positive goals can you set for yourself?

DRAW ON YOUR INTERESTS AND STRENGTHS

To break the negative focus of attention underpinning our anxiety, we need to view things differently. We need to direct our thoughts away from what we fear and towards the positive.

Changing your goals is one way to do this. Another, closely related technique is to capitalise on your interests and strengths – to use them to help you look at the situations that trigger your anxiety from a more optimistic perspective.

We recently came across a fantastic illustration of this technique. Lucy sought out the help of a therapist because of problems at work. She believed that her colleagues were all more intelligent, and better at their jobs, than she was. With such a low opinion of herself, talking to colleagues could be a very stressful experience.

In particular, the many social occasions organised by the company had become a nightmare for her. As each occasion approached, Lucy's anxiety would increase. Convinced that her colleagues must look down on her, and that every time she opened her mouth she'd show why they were right to do so, she would hover on the margins, doing her best to avoid being drawn into a conversation and constantly checking her watch to find out how much more she would have to endure. Many of Lucy's colleagues assumed that she preferred her own company and left her to it – which only reinforced Lucy's belief that they didn't like her.

In the course of one of their chats, the therapist had discovered that Lucy was an avid bird-watcher. So he suggested that she apply her ornithological skills to the social occasions that made her so anxious. He wasn't, of course, asking her to spend the evening scanning the room for peregrine falcons. Not literally, anyway. What he had in mind was that she should imagine the people around her as birds. When she observed them carefully, which birds did they most remind her of? Who was a sparrow and who was an eagle? Who were the songbirds and who was more like the chattering jackdaw? Who were the brightly coloured parakeets and birds of paradise?

The idea worked brilliantly. It switched Lucy's attention away from her imagined failings and redirected it outwards towards the people she was with. But when she looked at her colleagues, it wasn't in order to confirm her fears. Instead she was observing them from a completely different perspective – and, because bird-watching was a source of so much pleasure for Lucy, it was a perspective that had only positive associations for her. Suddenly, she felt in control of the situation. Her anxiety receded. And she found it far easier to chat to her colleagues.

Could you apply this technique to your own anxiety? Can you think of ways in which you can use your interests and strengths to help shift your focus of attention? Maybe you're a keen reader, or you love movies. Perhaps you're really into clothes, or music.

When you find yourself in a situation that makes you anxious, you could concentrate on what people are wearing, or which characters they remind you of, or which piece of music would best suit a soundtrack for the scene.

Sceptical? Wondering whether this could work for you? Well, why not conduct an experiment? The next time you're anxious about something, focus on the negative aspects of the situation. Let your fear determine your goals, so that your objective is simply to avoid harm. On the occasion after that, try switching your attention to the positive. Then ask yourself: which worked best? Was shifting your attention helpful? Did it lower your anxiety? Did it make it easier for you to cope?

(You can use this compare and contrast tactic for pretty much all of the techniques in this book, though bear in mind that many of them will become increasingly effective with practice. If you don't notice a big improvement first time around, don't be discouraged. Keep going and you'll get there.)

DEVELOP YOUR CURIOSITY

A couple of years ago we interviewed the actor Michael Palin for another book we were writing about anxiety. We were keen to find out how he dealt with the nerves that we assumed must be an occupational hazard for most actors and presenters.

Our hunch was correct. Palin told us he had rarely met a performer who didn't suffer from nerves. He was no exception, but he did manage to cope pretty well with his anxiety. Helping him to do so was a striking curiosity about the world, an appetite for experience and a sense that, as he put it, 'everything matters'.

Michael Palin's experience chimes with what psychologists have discovered: people who are curious about life tend to be happier than those who are not. This may be partly because their attention is focused externally – rather than dwelling on how they feel inside, they engage with what is outside. For these individuals, life is a rich source of pleasure and interest. Why, then, waste time on gloomy introspection?

Curiosity comes easily for some, but don't worry if you're not among them: you can train yourself to be more curious. It's a skill – and skills can always be learned.

Practise turning your attention away from your anxious thoughts and towards the world around you. You can do this wherever you happen to be – in the shower, taking the bus to work, in the office or at home, when you're shopping or out and about with friends and family. Pause. Slow your breathing. Look around. Inhabit the moment as fully as you can. Try to take in every little detail: the colours, the textures, the sounds, the smells. Aim to find at least one thing you've never noticed before.

Let your imagination wander. Find the magic in what you see. Allow yourself to wonder why things are as they seem. Why are the leaves on that tree shaped as they are? What did this place look like before these offices were built? Where is that person hurrying to? What are they thinking? What is their life like? If you could change one thing in the scene, what would it be? If you could take home one tiny part of what you see, what would you choose? What will you try to always remember?

> *Spend a few minutes each day cultivating your curiosity and eventually it will become a habit.*

Spend a few minutes each day cultivating your curiosity and eventually it will become a habit. No longer will you need to remind yourself to look around: it will happen automatically. Then you'll find that you're spending much less time worrying and more time engaging with the world around you. The balance of your attention will have shifted, from in to out.

MAKE TIME FOR FLOW

What's the secret of happiness? This is a question that increasing numbers of psychologists have tried to answer in recent years. As you might expect, there's no simple answer: well-being is almost always the result of a combination of factors – one of which is often something called 'flow'.

So what is this miraculous thing called 'flow'? Well, it's what we experience when we're totally absorbed in an activity. And that's most likely to happen if we're doing something challenging (though not so difficult that we get discouraged). For example, we might be playing a musical instrument, painting or writing, or trying to solve a puzzle of some kind.

One of the amazing things about flow is what it does to our attention. For most of the day our mind flits around. We may be trying to focus on what we're doing at the moment, but we also find ourselves thinking about what we're going to do later, and what has happened to us in the past. If we're feeling low or anxious, it can feel as though we're 'living in our head', constantly mulling over what we take to be past mistakes and worrying about possible problems in the future.

But flow activities put a stop to all of this. Our attention becomes entirely focused on the task in hand. Time seems to stop – afterwards we may be amazed to discover that an hour or more has gone by. We're suddenly oblivious to what is going on around us: the outside world melts away. And we lose our sense of self. The usual confusion of thoughts, feelings and worries is suspended. Now all that matters is what we're *doing*.

Which activities produce flow for you? If you're struggling to come up with any, think back – right to childhood, if necessary. Draw up a list. And then ensure you build these activities into your weekly routine.

Anxiety monopolises our attention. It's rather like a powerful magnet, drawing all thoughts towards itself. Our view of the world changes, so that we see only danger and disaster.

But when we learn to shift our focus of attention, we undermine our anxiety. Give the techniques in this chapter a try. Concentrate on the positive. Cultivate your curiosity. Lose yourself in activity. And you'll feel calmer, more confident and more content.

CHAPTER 9

Boosting positive feelings

To really get the better of troublesome emotions like anxiety, we need to use a two-pronged strategy.

The first approach is relatively straightforward: we tackle our anxious thoughts directly, using the techniques we've set out in previous chapters. The second is a little more devious. This time, we reduce our negative feelings by *increasing* our positive feelings. We weaken our anxiety by boosting our happiness. In this chapter we're going to show you how.

FIVE A DAY FOR HAPPINESS

How can we improve our mental health? How can we raise our level of well-being? And how can we stop psychological problems such as anxiety taking root?

Those were the questions the UK government put to more than 400 experts in 2008. The result was a 'five a day' programme for happiness – five key activities we can undertake in order to improve our mood. Here's what those experts recommended.

Connect
Psychologists have known for a while that the quality of our relationships with other people can have a major bearing on

our happiness. We humans are social creatures. And even those of us who are often content with our own company need to know there are people who love, like and care for us.

So make time for the people who matter to you. Life being what it is, it's easy for the fun stuff to get squeezed out by work and domestic chores. If that's a problem for you, fight back! Make an arrangement with your partner, family or friends and schedule it into your diary. And ensure that you've always got something lined up to look forward to.

Be physically active

We're all aware that exercise will help us stay physically healthy. But now there's increasing evidence that it can boost our psychological well-being, too.

Exactly what form of exercise you take doesn't much matter. What you're looking for is an activity that gives your cardiovascular system – your heart and lungs – a proper workout. That might be jogging, cycling, swimming, playing football, dancing or badminton, for example. But if you're not sporty, an energetic session of gardening, housework or brisk walking will also do the job.

Aim to be physically active for at least 30 minutes several times a week. If you haven't exercised for a few years, it's sensible to build up gradually: aim for 20 minutes three times a week and progress from there.

Be curious

As we discovered in Chapter 8, people who are happy seem to have the knack of finding something of interest in even the most ordinary aspects of life. But even if curiosity doesn't come naturally, there's a lot we can do to develop it – for a reminder of how to cultivate your curiosity, turn to page 90.

Learn

Apparently, most breeds of shark must keep swimming in order to stay alive. If they stop moving, they can't breathe. In this respect the shark reminds us a little of human beings. We, too, need to keep moving – not in order to keep breathing, of course, but to stay happy. We need to feel that we're progressing, that we're developing our skills and abilities – that we are, in short, *learning*.

It feels so good to master a new skill. In fact, you don't need to wait that long: it feels great just to be trying something new and to realise that you're steadily becoming more competent at something that engages you. And if you're learning alongside other people – at an evening class, for example – you'll have the enjoyment that comes with social contact, too.

So ask yourself: *what would I like to learn today?* And then go for it!

Give

The evidence is clear: people who help others – who give their time, attention and energy – are happier than individuals who simply look after number one.

Researchers in Germany tracked the happiness of several thousand adults over a number of years. They found that individuals who had made helping others a priority were much more content than those who hadn't. (The same study, incidentally, also highlighted the importance for happiness of relationships, and of involvement in social and political activities. Money, status and possessions turned out to be relatively insignificant for well-being.)

Spend a few moments now thinking about the five a day for happiness. How do you measure up? Which of the five are you strongest at? And which do you think you could do more of? Once you've identified an area that you'd like to work on, aim to add a relevant activity to your routine.

What if you're struggling to come up with something suitable? Well, you can ask the people close to you: what works for them? Which activities do they think might suit you? Cast your mind back: what have you really enjoyed doing in the past? To help you generate ideas, ask yourself the following questions:

- ★ What could I do for an afternoon that I'd really find fun or satisfying?
- ★ What could I do for an hour?
- ★ Is there something good I could plan to do one weekend?
- ★ What can I do that costs money?
- ★ What can I do for free?
- ★ What could I do that would really stimulate my mind?
- ★ What would give me a sense of achievement?
- ★ Is there a course or evening class I'd find interesting?
- ★ What physical activity would I like to do?
- ★ What about learning a practical skill?
- ★ If a friend was visiting, what would I suggest we do?

- ★ Do I want to meet new people?
- ★ Do I want to make new friends?
- ★ What enjoyable activity could I do on my own?
- ★ What could I do at home?
- ★ Where would I like to go?
- ★ What could I do that I've never done before?
- ★ What have I enjoyed doing in the past?
- ★ Are there any interesting events or activities listed in the paper?
- ★ Could I just get some lists of what classes are available, to give me ideas?
- ★ Where else could I look for inspiration? The library? The internet? Tourist information?
- ★ How about voluntary work?

Making any change to our normal lifestyle can take some getting used to. So, as with all the exercises in this book, it's best to proceed gradually. Aim to introduce one new five-a-day activity at a time. Move on only when you've integrated it into your routine.

Imagine, for example, that you're keen both to learn a new skill *and* to get fit. It's probably wise not to start a running programme and an Italian language evening class at the same time. Give one (let's say it's the running) your full attention. Once you're used to exercising three times a week – once running is a part of your life – you can think about adding an Italian class to your weekly commitments.

Now let's look at some more proven techniques for improving mood. Underlying each is the idea that, when we're feeling anxious or sad, we tend to notice the things that seem to confirm our negative feelings and disregard those that don't – which only reinforces our low mood. Yet if we focus on the positive things in life, our mood will lift.

WHAT'S GOING RIGHT FOR ME RIGHT NOW?

This technique was pioneered by one of the leading psychologists of happiness, Barbara Fredrickson. The idea is very simple – you simply ask yourself one question: *what's going right for me right now?* Then you find the positives in your current situation.

When we're anxious or stressed this may not be as straightforward as it sounds. If we're finding things tough, it's easy to feel that there's nothing good going on in our life; our view of the world is completely coloured by our worries. But we need to look more closely.

Perhaps the positives stem from something as ordinary as the weather, or the fact that we've just enjoyed a delicious cup of tea. Maybe our football team won on Saturday, or our favourite TV programme is about to start a new series. If we stick at it, we might remember that we are fortunate to have a loving partner, great friends, a supportive family.

Whether we come up with something weighty or trivial isn't really important. What matters is that by practising this exercise regularly we train ourselves to see the positive. When we do that, we have an emotional reaction: we feel happier. And, like a seesaw, when we boost our positive emotions our negative feelings – our stress and worry and anxiety – lose some of their power over us.

SAVOURING

The 'what's going right for me right now?' exercise is a great way to learn to savour the moment – to notice, relish and celebrate the good things in life. But savouring isn't simply a skill we can apply to the present. We can also learn to appreciate, and delight in, the past and the future.

> *If we learn to savour, we can rekindle that pleasure.*

Imagine, for example, that you've recently returned from a fabulous holiday. You had a wonderful time while you were away, but now you're back in the old routine. Sadly, the fun of the holiday seems well and truly over. But if we learn to savour, we can rekindle that pleasure.

How do we do it? We deliberately recall our holiday. We look at photos and videos. We reminisce with the friends who travelled with us. We try to picture in our mind, as vividly and completely as possible, the sights we saw; we deliberately summon up the sounds, the smells, the feel of the sea water on our skin.

By remembering our holiday like this, we prolong the happiness it gave us. Sure, we'd probably prefer to be back there for real. But savouring means that the experience isn't lost to us. It isn't simply swallowed up with the passing of time. Instead, it can be a source of pleasure whenever we choose to seek it.

We can do something similar with events that haven't happened yet. If you have something nice planned, make sure you spend time actively looking forward to it. Indulge yourself in daydreams. Imagine the fun you're going to have – you'll find it's a great way to calm your anxiety and boost your mood.

KEEP A GRATITUDE DIARY

Why are some people happier than others? That question has generated an extraordinary amount of research in recent years (happiness is one of the hottest topics in psychology right now). One of the striking conclusions to emerge from this research is that happy people tend to be more grateful than other individuals.

By gratitude, we're not really talking about manners. It's not so much that happy people are more polite. No, this is a deeper, more fundamental gratitude. It's an approach to life. It's about recognising and appreciating the positive aspects of our existence. It means understanding how much we have to be thankful for, whatever our personal situation.

When we look at gratitude like this, we can see why it's so closely linked to happiness. Gratitude helps us to focus on the good things in life. It tunes us into the positive. And that, inevitably, raises our mood.

Of course, you might not be feeling especially grateful at the moment. When we're anxious and stressed and worried, we might wonder what exactly we have to be thankful for. But if we deliberately practise being grateful, our view of the world will shift.

Each night for two weeks, sit down with a pen and paper and think of five things for which you are grateful. Sound impossible?

Think you'll struggle to come up with anything at all, let alone five examples? You'll be surprised. Stick with it and you'll soon start to notice the positive aspects to your life. And remember, those positives can be as big or as small as you like. For example:

- ★ Good day at work; got lots done.
- ★ Really nice email from my friend. Was so nice to hear from her.
- ★ Did my piano practice, even though I was tired. Think I'm definitely improving.
- ★ Alice seems to be enjoying school at last: such a relief!
- ★ No more chores to do this evening. Looking forward to finally watching that DVD.

When the two weeks are up, it's time to reflect on the experience. Have you enjoyed keeping your gratitude diary? Has it helped you to be more receptive to the good stuff? Have you noticed your mood brighten?

If you've found it a useful exercise, you may want to make the gratitude diary a regular part of your routine. Every night may not suit you; you might prefer to update your diary once, twice or three times a week. But whatever you go for, try to stick to your schedule. That way the diary will become a habit.

WHAT'S GOOD ABOUT ME?

Right now you may assume the answer to that question is 'not much'. That's understandable: if you're feeling anxious, it's bound to affect your mood. Your opinion of the world, and of yourself, may well take a bit of a battering. But don't believe your own negative publicity.

> *Don't believe your own negative publicity.*

Make a list now of the positive things about yourself. What do you value in yourself? What do you think other people like about you? What are you proud of?

If you're struggling to come up with anything much, take a look at the following table. It lists 24 character strengths identified by the Values in Action Institute, an organisation set up by a number of leading psychologists. (If you like, you can assess your strengths by taking the VIA questionnaire at **http://uat. viacharacter.org**.)

Creativity	Curiosity
Love of learning	Judgement and open-mindedness
Perspective	Authenticity/genuineness/honesty
Bravery	Persistence/perseverance
Zest/energy/wholeheartedness	Kindness
Love	Social intelligence (being sensitive to other people's needs and desires)
Fairness	Leadership
Teamwork	Forgiveness/mercy
Modesty/humility	Prudence
Self-regulation/self-control	Appreciation of beauty and excellence
Gratitude	Hope
Humour	Religiousness/spirituality

We're willing to bet that your list might be a little longer now. What's good about you? So much. Far more than you give yourself credit for.

RECORDING THE POSITIVES

Here's another exercise to help us pick up on the positive things in life.

For a week, we want you to keep a diary of the good things that happen to you each day. You can jot things down as they occur to you. Or it may be more practical to set aside a little time every evening.

You don't have to write a lot – a few words will do for each entry. Simply make a note of the event and how it made you feel.

Day	Positive thing	How did you feel?

The important thing is that you're turning your thoughts away from your worries and fears and towards the parts of your life that make you happy. (As we saw in Chapter 8, changing the focus of your attention like this can be a great way to overcome anxiety. It's also a brilliant method for increasing well-being.)

To give you a sense of the kind of thing to aim for, here's a day from the diary compiled by Rebecca, a 39-year-old public relations consultant:

Day	Positive thing	How did you feel?
Wednesday	My day to take the kids to school.	Really happy to do the walk with them and to see the other mums.
	Bus actually turned up on time!	Relaxed – even managed to read a bit of my book rather than sitting there checking my watch as I usually do.
	Constructive phone call with clients. Managed to pin down exactly what they need from us.	Pleased with myself, and looking forward to getting on with the project.
	Alison turned up with a coffee for me.	Surprised and grateful!
	Lunchtime meeting cancelled. Decided to get out in the sun for a walk instead.	Was great to get out of the office for a while. Beautiful weather. Suddenly felt very calm and optimistic.
	Jessica brought in her newborn.	Fantastic to see Jessica looking so happy and well. And her baby is very cute.
	Came home to find Rob had already given the kids their baths and even washed their hair.	Fortunate to have escaped that particular chore! And thankful to Rob.
	Phone call with my mum. She's finally over that chest infection.	Relieved.
	Watched favourite thriller on TV with Rob. Didn't think about work once.	Totally absorbed in the programme. Relaxed. Happy.

At the end of the week, take some time out and read back over your diary. Notice just how many good things have happened in the past seven days. And remember the way your mood lifted as each occurred.

Sometimes life seems like just a succession of problems, worries, stresses and fears. But when we keep a diary of the positives, we're able to look at things from a different perspective. We're reminded of the many good things in our world. We get better at spotting them in the future. And we feel happier.

CHAPTER 10

Relaxing body and mind

If we asked you to think of five terms to describe what it feels like to be anxious, which would you opt for? Here are some of the suggestions we received when we asked around:

★ Edgy

★ Tense

★ Apprehensive

★ Distracted

★ Burdened

★ Fearful

★ Miserable

★ Agitated

★ Nervous

★ Flustered.

What about the opposite of these adjectives? You might think, for example, of *calm, relaxed, peaceful, tranquil, content* – exactly the qualities that each of the strategies we've described so far in this book sets out to achieve.

This calmness, this feeling of peace, is also the primary objective of a set of relaxation techniques, some of which – like yoga and meditation – are thousands of years old. They are exercises that are specifically designed to produce a deep relaxation of the body and mind. It's these exercises that we're going to focus on now.

It's a good idea to give all of them a try – that way you'll be able to find out what works best for you. Aim to devote at least a little time each day to your chosen relaxation exercise: around 10–20 minutes will do it. The key thing is that it becomes a part of your daily routine.

Many people find it helpful – and fun – to practise activities like yoga and meditation in a group. If you think this might be right for you, you should be able to find a class nearby. If that isn't possible, or you prefer to forge ahead alone, you'll find no shortage of books, CDs, DVDs and websites to guide you.

PROGRESSIVE MUSCLE RELAXATION

When we're feeling anxious, the turmoil and tension of our thoughts are mirrored in our body. Our muscles tighten, our heart rate increases and our breathing becomes faster and shallower.

To calm this physical tension, the US doctor Edmund Jacobson (1888–1983) developed a technique called *progressive muscle relaxation*. The idea is that each group of muscles in your body is tensed and released in turn. Once you've tensed the muscle consciously, it's much easier to then consciously relax it. You can follow the order of muscles outlined here, or vary the pattern if you prefer. The key point is to gradually progress around your body and to include a good range of the major muscles.

Choose a time and place when you know you won't be disturbed. Make yourself comfortable. Take off your shoes; loosen any tight clothing. Sit in a chair or, if you're confident you won't fall asleep, lie down on the floor, or on a bed or sofa. Close your eyes.

For a minute or so, concentrate on breathing deeply and slowly. Feel your body begin to relax.

Clench both fists as tightly as you can. Count to 10 and then release. Enjoy the relaxation of your muscles for approximately 20 seconds, then move on to the next exercise.

Tense the muscles in your neck and shoulders by lifting your shoulders up to your ears. Again, hold for 10 seconds and then relax for 20 seconds.

Moving on to the muscles in your face, press your teeth together as firmly as you can. At the same time, keep your eyelids tightly closed. Hold for 10 seconds and relax for the standard 20 seconds.

Now focus on your chest. Take a deep breath and, after counting to 10, exhale gently.

Clench your stomach muscles, hold for a count of 10, then release.

Now it's time to work on your feet and legs. Press down with your legs. Then flex your toes upwards to work your calf muscles. Finally, pull your toes downwards to tense the muscles in your feet. For all three manoeuvres, hold for 10 seconds and then release for 20 seconds.

Enjoy the steady rhythm of your breathing.

When you've completed this cycle of exercises, let yourself rest. Notice how the tension has left your body. Savour the feeling of deep relaxation that has taken its place. Enjoy the steady rhythm of your breathing. If you detect any tightness in your body, flex the muscles in question and then release.

Aim to spend about 10 minutes each day on progressive muscle relaxation. Find a convenient time – perhaps first thing in the morning or when you arrive home from work – and make it a regular date.

YOGA

You can certainly practise yoga on your own: there are dozens – perhaps hundreds – of books and other resources to help you. But it's best to take the plunge and join a class. You'll learn fast. You'll know that you're going about things in the right way. And you may well make some new friends.

Attending a class may seem scary. But you can bet that you'll be pleasantly surprised – and proud of yourself, too. Remember that yoga isn't a competitive activity: no one will be trying to outdo you. In fact, no one – other than the teacher – will be paying any attention to what you're doing: they'll all be too busy with the exercises themselves. You should be able to find a class that's right for your level of experience and mobility and, if that's what you'd prefer, for men or women only.

MINDFULNESS

Mindfulness is hugely popular right now, both as a general relaxation technique and as a specific treatment for anxiety and depression. The evidence suggests that it really can make a huge – and hugely positive – difference to our well-being. In fact, recent research has shown that it can actually produce positive changes in our brain.

Mindfulness was developed by blending Western psychology with ancient Buddhist beliefs and practice, and especially meditation. This is how it's been defined by four of its pioneers, Mark Williams, John Teasdale, Zindel Segal and Jon Kabat-Zinn:

> *Mindfulness is the awareness that arises from paying attention on purpose, in the present moment, non-judgementally, to things as they are. Mindfulness is not paying more attention but paying attention differently and more wisely – with the whole mind and heart, using the full resources of the body and its sense.* (*The Mindful Way Through Depression*, 2007)

When we practise mindfulness, we focus all our energies on the present moment – on how things are right now. We aren't bogged down in memories of the past or worries about the future. Instead we understand that thoughts are just passing mental events; they come and go, like clouds across a sky. And they aren't necessarily true or reliable or even at all meaningful. (You can see how this might be especially useful for people who are struggling with anxious thoughts.)

The raisin meditation

This exercise will provide you with a quick introduction to mindfulness. All you need is five minutes to yourself and a few raisins. If you don't like raisins, feel free to use something else – perhaps a piece of fruit, or a biscuit, or a square of chocolate. Your aim is to experience that item of food as fully as you possibly can.

Begin by picking up a raisin. For about 20 seconds, concentrate on how it *feels* in your hand, its texture and weight, the sensations it produces in contact with your skin.

Then focus on how the raisin *looks*. Try to take in every detail, as if you were studying a rare and precious jewel. Again, spend about 20 seconds on this stage (and on the others that follow).

Hold the raisin to your nose. How does it *smell*? Breathe deeply; savour the raisin's scent.

Next, carefully place the raisin *on your tongue*. Let it rest there while you notice exactly how it feels. Then gently examine the raisin with your tongue.

Begin to *chew* the raisin. Do it slowly and focus your attention on the taste and texture. How does your mouth feel? How would you describe this experience to someone who had never tasted a raisin?

When you're ready, gradually *swallow* the raisin. Again, try to register every last detail of the process. Concentrate as if you were performing the most intricate manoeuvre rather than simply swallowing some dried fruit.

Lastly, think about how it feels now that you've swallowed the raisin. Can you still taste it? Do you detect its scent? What sensations do you notice in your mouth and teeth?

What did you make of the experience as a whole? Did you notice a new intensity to the relatively humdrum act of eating a raisin? Did you feel your awareness blossom into life? This intensity, this awareness, is mindfulness in action.

PRACTISING MINDFULNESS

In the remainder of this chapter we present a number of other mindfulness meditation exercises. Aim to practise at least one of them each day. *But I don't have the time!* you might be thinking. Actually, none of them will take more than a few minutes. That's a pretty small investment for what many people find is a big upturn in their mood.

Once you've tried mindfulness, we think you'll gladly find the time. It's a wonderful way to step back from the rush of daily life, to experience a precious stillness, to find calmness amidst the chaos.

Even better, you can take mindfulness into your everyday activities. You'll learn that you can meditate, even if it's just for a minute or two, in virtually any situation. And that means you'll be able to increase your feelings of calmness no matter where you are or what you're doing.

You'll be able to increase your feelings of calmness no matter where you are or what you're doing.

A breathing meditation

This is a great meditation for beginners – and for everyone else, too. You have just one aim: to concentrate on your breathing.

Begin by making yourself comfortable in your meditation position. The classic meditating pose is seated on the floor or a cushion with your legs crossed. Of course, that isn't comfortable for everyone – for example, those of us with bad backs!

What you're after is a position that you can maintain for 10 or 20 minutes without discomfort. If you're unhappy with your position it will only distract you from your meditation. Ideally, your back will be straight and your posture upright.

If sitting on your bottom on the floor isn't right for you, try a firm, straight-backed chair. Kneeling can be good, too, as long as your knees are up to it. Position a cushion between your bottom and your feet.

If sitting isn't possible for you, don't worry. You can meditate standing up, walking or lying down. As ever, it's good to experiment and discover the position that suits you best.

Wear loose, comfortable clothing. As with all the relaxation exercises in this chapter, it's crucial that you aren't disturbed. Trying to meditate while your children yell for attention, or your housemate sings along to the radio, or the cat miaows for food, is taking optimism a step too far! So find that secluded spot and make the next 10 minutes all your own.

When you're ready to begin, close your eyes and direct your attention to the rise and fall of your breathing. Observe how your body behaves when you inhale and exhale: how your abdomen gradually rises and falls; the sensation in your nostrils; the feeling in your lungs and chest.

Notice the rhythm of your breathing. Let your mind focus on the cycle of inhalation and exhalation, the breath in and the breath out.

You may find that your breathing becomes deeper and more regular during the meditation. If that happens, great. If it doesn't, well, that's fine, too. Just let your breathing happen naturally. There's no need to alter it in any way.

Almost certainly you'll find that your mind wanders during the meditation. You might, for example, suddenly wonder what you're going to cook for supper tonight, or remember a remark someone made to you. Perhaps you'll worry that these interruptions mean you're not meditating 'correctly'.

Don't become disheartened if thoughts and feelings pop into your mind like this. It's absolutely normal, even for experienced meditators. Simply return your attention to your breathing – if necessary, over and over again.

Keep going with the meditation for about 10 minutes.

The body scan meditation

In this meditation we're going to direct our attention to the various parts of our body. As with all meditations, your first task is to make yourself comfortable. For this exercise it's best to be lying down. That could be on your bed, on a sofa, or even on the floor if that's what you prefer.

Ensure you won't be interrupted. This is another great reason to develop a meditation routine. By meditating at the same time each day – and in the same place – not only does it become a habit for you, the other people in your life understand that those 20 or 30 minutes are your private, personal time. This saves you having to explain for the umpteenth time that you don't want a cup of tea right now; you can't answer the phone when it rings; and you definitely aren't free to cook dinner/tidy up/unload the washing machine!

Begin the meditation by directing your attention to your body as a whole. Tune into the sensations in those parts of your body that touch the surface you're lying on – for example, the back of your head, your shoulders, buttocks, legs, heels. Feel the tension in your muscles and limbs ebb away.

Now turn your attention to your toes and feet. How do they feel? If you don't sense anything much, don't worry. If you notice aches and pains, don't be concerned. *What* you feel isn't important; your objective is simply to become aware of a particular area of your body.

In due course let your attention begin its travels around your body. Gradually move from your feet and toes to your ankles, then your calves, thighs, hips, genitals, stomach, chest, lungs, arms and hands. After your hands, switch your awareness to your neck, face and head. Spend as long as you like on each part of your body, though aim for a minimum of 15–20 seconds.

At each point in your journey, gently note the feeling in that part of your body. Don't try to analyse that feeling; don't try to change it. Simply let it fill your mind. If other thoughts pop up – and they often do – don't fight them. It's nothing to worry about. Merely direct your attention back to your body.

The meditation ends as it began. Turn your mind to your body as a whole. Again, don't analyse or judge or try to alter anything. Simply rest in awareness. Allow yourself to be borne along by the full swell of sensation. Give yourself up to the moment. And when you're ready, you can open your eyes, stretch and gently sit up.

Compassionate meditation

The aim of compassionate meditation is to develop your positive feelings for yourself, the people you know and those you will never meet. For many people, and perhaps especially men, it's more difficult than a breathing or body scan meditation. Openly expressing our emotions isn't something that comes naturally to lots of us. But do give this meditation a try. After all, no one else will know what you're thinking!

Imagine for a moment that you love yourself as deeply as you love your child or partner or best friend.

Now picture yourself experiencing heartfelt affection not simply for those closest to you but for the nameless people you pass in the street and even for the mass of humanity you have never encountered.

If we could feel like this, wouldn't we experience a wonderful sense of well-being? Wouldn't our days be filled with pleasure, enjoyment and contentment? Wouldn't the world seem a much happier place than it sometimes does today? This vision is the driving force behind compassionate (or loving-kindness) meditation.

Begin the meditation by tuning into the rhythm of your breathing and the sensations of your body. When you're relaxed and ready, visualise a person you have loved deeply and who has loved you. Think back to the times you spent with them and how their love made you feel.

Try to recall a particular moment in as much detail as you can. Let yourself experience once again the emotions you felt then: the love, contentment and joy. In your mind, communicate your love to the person you have chosen. Allow the warmth of your affection to radiate out towards them.

Many people find it helpful during this meditation to express their love through words. You could say to yourself versions of traditional Buddhist phrases: 'May they be safe. May they be happy. May they be free from suffering. May they be peaceful.' Alternatively, choose something that is especially meaningful to you.

> *Remember: you are entitled to your love. You deserve your love.*

Now direct that love – and those compassionate words – towards yourself. If you find this difficult, awkward or embarrassing, keep going. It will become easier. Remember: you are entitled to your love. *You deserve your love.*

Then, in turn, bring to mind someone you know well and care for, a person you see occasionally but have no feelings for, and someone who has annoyed or upset you in the past. To each of these individuals, reach out with love and compassion. Feel the waves of your loving-kindness emanating from your heart. Bask in this warmth.

Finally, let your love embrace every living being on the planet. To help you do this, try visualising the Earth and, while you do so, repeat your compassionate phrases. Enjoy your feelings of love. Savour the contentment they have inspired in you. Delight in these sensations for as long as you choose.

The three-minute breathing space meditation

In many ways this is the perfect meditation: all it requires is three minutes of your time. It was developed by Mark Williams, John Teasdale, Zindel Segal and Jon Kabat-Zinn, all of whom have made a huge contribution to the development of mindfulness techniques.

The meditation is structured in three parts. Your focus will move from your thoughts and feelings to your breathing and finally to your whole body.

You can do this meditation sitting or standing (but preferably not lying down). Hold yourself upright, though make sure it's a position you can adopt comfortably for the duration of the meditation.

For the first minute or so, focus your attention on your thoughts, feelings and physical sensations. What are you thinking? Which emotions can you detect? How does your body feel?

Don't analyse your thoughts and feelings. Don't attempt to change them. Simply experience them. Awareness is all.

In the second part of the meditation, concentrate on your breathing. Follow the steady rise and fall of your chest and diaphragm as you inhale and exhale. If you become distracted, simply guide your mind back to your breathing.

For the third and final minute, broaden your awareness so that you notice how your whole body feels when you breathe. Once again, don't judge these physical sensations – there is no right or wrong way to be feeling. But if you detect any unpleasant sensations, direct your attention to them. Don't try to make these feelings disappear; instead acknowledge and accept their presence in this moment.

Try practising the breathing space meditation twice a day for a week, or whenever you're feeling anxious, worried, stressed or sad.

CHAPTER 11

Improving your sleep

Pity the giraffe. No other mammal gets so little sleep. The giraffe manages just two hours a night. (And those two hours aren't even continuous – giraffes tend to sleep in blocks of about 60 minutes.)

Why are giraffes so sleep-deprived? Well, scientists believe it's because lying down leaves them vulnerable to predators. As you might imagine, 20-foot-tall giraffes can't simply spring to their feet – getting up is a laborious, time-consuming process. So they prefer to spend as much time as possible upright. (Under the circumstances, you might think that it would be sensible for giraffes to get all, or at least most, of their sleep while standing. But though sleeping upright isn't unknown among giraffes, it is relatively unusual.)

So the giraffe's sleep habits are a response to potential danger. The longer a giraffe dozes, the greater the likelihood that it will end up as a meal for a hungry lion. Who would sleep well under that kind of pressure? It's a wonder the poor animal is able to nod off at all.

As it happens, the giraffe's situation isn't so very different from that of anxious humans. The giraffe doesn't sleep for long because of possible threat, and the same goes for anxious people. When we're very worried or fearful, we don't sleep well because we can't relax. And we can't relax because we're on edge, waiting for something bad to happen. We're hyperalert.

> *When we're very worried or fearful, we don't sleep well because we can't relax.*

But though not sleeping much is useful for giraffes, it doesn't tend to help humans. The danger we fear generally isn't going to leap on us in the dark. And usually, of course, what we're worried about is unlikely to happen at all.

If you've suffered from insomnia – the medical term for sleeplessness – you'll know just how stressful it can be. Most adults need around seven to eight hours' sleep a night. When we repeatedly fall short of this, the impact on our mood and our ability to function normally can be enormous. We'll feel depressed. We'll be touchy and irritable. We'll feel stressed and anxious. And if we're already struggling with anxiety, those feelings are likely to be even more intense.

Unfortunately, anxious people can sometimes fall into a cycle of sleeplessness. They struggle to get the sleep they need because they're so keyed up. But being tired only increases their anxiety, which makes it even more difficult to sleep. And so on. It's not surprising, then, that a high percentage of people who are struggling with anxiety are also suffering from sleep problems.

STRATEGIES FOR TACKLING SLEEPLESSNESS: STAGE 1

If you're having problems sleeping, you are most definitely not alone. In fact, on any given night, around a third of adults in the UK are thought to experience insomnia, with women twice as likely to be affected as men.

When we're lying awake at 3am, or battling to keep our eyes open the next day, it can seem as if sleeplessness is a life sentence. We may feel that things will never improve; that a decent night's sleep is a thing of the past.

But it doesn't have to be like this. There are now many well-researched, highly effective remedies for insomnia – strategies that have been proven to work, time and time again. And you can put these strategies into practice yourself. Here's how to go about it.

Make sleep a priority

For many of us, life is so full of demands and tasks and chores that there just don't seem to be enough hours in the day. We're struggling frantically to juggle work commitments and domestic responsibilities, and sleep can seem like a luxury we can't afford. It's a big mistake.

Try not to let sleep be squeezed out of your life by other pressures. Instead, make it a priority in your life. This is especially important if you're suffering from insomnia. Put sleep first. Implement the steps we're going to describe in the next few pages. When you do, you'll soon feel calmer, happier and less anxious. (And if you happen to be trying to lose weight, as many of us are, recent research suggests that getting a good night's sleep will make a significant difference.) These techniques really will help – but you have to give them a chance.

Exercise every day

Everyone knows that exercise is good for our health. But we may not realise that it can also have a really positive effect on our ability to sleep.

The reason is simple: when we've been for a brisk walk or a run, or played a game of badminton, or worked out in the gym, we'll inevitably feel tired. And if our body is tired – and not simply our mind – we're more likely to sleep. There's also good evidence that being out in the sunshine and fresh air during the day can help us sleep better at night.

> *If our body is tired – and not simply our mind – we're more likely to sleep.*

But there is one exception to the rule: don't exercise late in the evening. It'll make you feel more alert just at the time when you need to be winding down for the night.

Cut out caffeine, nicotine and alcohol in the evening

If you're a smoker, we're sure you won't need (or want) us to lecture you on the evils of nicotine. But we will at least suggest that you refrain at night.

This is because nicotine is a stimulant. Smokers often believe that it's relaxing them, but in fact it has the opposite effect on our body. Nicotine gees us up physiologically. It raises our blood pressure. It puts us on edge. And it makes it more difficult to sleep.

The situation is exactly the same with caffeine. Drink a cup of coffee in the evening and you may well find that your mind and body are still buzzing hours later. Remember, too, that caffeine isn't only found in coffee: it's also present in tea and many cola and energy drinks.

Alcohol, meanwhile, has the opposite effect. Rather than being a stimulant, alcohol is a depressant. This doesn't necessarily mean that it makes us feel sad, but rather that it slows and dampens down our physiological reactions.

The first thing alcohol slows down is the parts of the brain that make us feel inhibited, stressed or anxious. Now these effects are a big part of the reason why alcohol is so popular (and has been for tens of thousands of years). And it explains why drink may be especially attractive to people trying to cope with anxiety and other psychological problems such as depression: they need a lift. But though alcohol may make us feel better temporarily, in the long run it tends to intensify those negative emotions. It also interferes with the quality of our sleep.

You may have noticed that when you've had a drink you fall asleep faster than usual. But you probably also wake up more often during the night. The overall quality of your sleep is worse. And you don't feel so rested in the morning. That's because we're all programmed to follow a five-stage sleep cycle. Alcohol disrupts this cycle. If you've drunk a lot you're also likely to wake up feeling thirsty or unwell or because you need to use the loo.

Develop a relaxing evening routine

Parents are often advised that, if they want their little ones to fall asleep promptly at bedtime, they should implement a relaxing evening routine, usually involving a bath and then a book. Nothing much changes when we become adults. We still need to wind down, to ease our mind and body through the transition from activity to rest.

Exactly how you do that is up to you – everyone will have their own preferences. But the old bath/book combination is definitely worth a try. Perhaps listen to calming music, or practise one of the relaxation and meditation exercises listed in Chapter 10.

Keep the light and noise levels low. Experiment and see what suits you best. Whatever you go for, aim to start your wind-down routine about half an hour before bed.

Just as important as what you do during this routine is what you *don't* do. Steer clear of any activity that's going to leave you anxious, stressed or just plain awake. So don't schedule your run for last thing at night. Resist the temptation to surf the internet or to check your email or text messages. And definitely don't do any work. Whatever it is, it can wait till morning. You have clocked off!

Eat a bedtime snack

The key word here is 'snack'. Even if you're feeling peckish, keep it plain and keep it small: maybe a banana, a piece of whole-wheat toast, a glass of milk or some herbal tea. Have your snack about 30 minutes before bed.

This will help you sleep, but anything more substantial may have the opposite effect. Overdo it, and you may find yourself lying awake while your digestive system goes about its work.

Get your sleeping environment right

It's tough to sleep well if your bed is uncomfortable, if you're too hot or cold, or if it's noisy or light. So make sure your bedroom is set up with whatever you need for a good night's sleep. For example, if you're waking up too early in the summer, invest in some blackout curtains. Keep your bedroom at a temperature that suits you (18°C is usually about right). If your mattress isn't right, change it.

Of course, some of these alterations may cost money. If finances are tight, aim to tackle one problem at a time. Bear in mind, though, that you'll feel so much happier when you're sleeping better. And a new mattress or curtains will last for years. All in all, it will be money well spent.

STRATEGIES FOR TACKLING SLEEPLESSNESS: STAGE 2

When you make the changes we've just described, you may well find that your sleep problems become a thing of the past. But what if they don't? What can you do then?

Well, if things haven't improved enough, you can move on to stage 2. And within just a few days, you'll notice the difference. This time around you'll really crack it.

Cut out daytime naps

When we've had a rotten night's sleep, we may be sorely tempted to sneak a nap during the day. It will probably feel wonderful. But it may not be doing us as much good as we think.

This is because when we sleep, and how long we sleep for, is partly determined by how long it is since we last slept. If we've enjoyed an afternoon nap, we run the risk of feeling wide awake at just the time when we'd normally be winding down for bed.

The result? Another sleepless night, which makes it more likely that we'll nap the next day – and so it goes on … If we're not careful, we can find that our sleep pattern has been turned upside down. We're awake for much of the night and asleep for a sizeable part of the day – which probably won't fit well with our other commitments and responsibilities.

So if you're struggling to sleep properly at night, resist the urge to nap during the day. It may be tough in the short term, but the pay-off will definitely make it worthwhile. (However, if feeling sleepy is going to be unsafe – for example, if you're driving any distance – skipping a nap isn't wise. In these situations, it's obviously more important that you're awake and alert.)

Get up at the same time each day and don't lie in

Yes, we can imagine what you're thinking when you read this one! The weekend lie-in is something lots of us look forward to all week. But if we're not sleeping well at night, we need to try something different.

Lie-ins can be problematic for the same reason as naps. They mean that we're sleeping at the 'wrong' time, and consequently we are awake at the wrong time, too.

The thought of going without a lie-in is unlikely to make your heart leap with joy. But it's only temporary. Once you've sorted out your sleep problem – and chances are it will take only a few days of concerted action – you can occasionally lie in for as long as you like.

For the moment, though, you should aim to get up at the same time each morning – say 7am or 8am. You need to do this even if, as is quite likely, you still feel tired. Because this way you're more likely to sleep well at night.

Learn to associate your bed with sleep

Marcel Proust wrote a million-word novel from his bed. John Lennon and Yoko Ono campaigned for peace from theirs. Virtually everyone we know seems to browse the web, answer their email and watch movies in bed.

> *We need to simplify the equation so that bed simply equals sleep and nothing else.*

As long as we're sleeping well, it doesn't matter what other activities we use our bed for. But if we're struggling with insomnia, we need to refocus. We need to simplify the equation so that bed simply equals sleep and nothing else. Otherwise, our mind and body will associate being in bed with activity rather than rest – and that's an association we'll need to break.

So until you're sleeping well again, that means no reading in bed. No eating or watching TV. No writing a diary. No using your laptop or mobile phone. Just sleep. (Actually, there is one exception: sex is okay because it usually leaves people feeling sleepy.)

Go to bed only when you're tired
If you're not tired, there's absolutely no point in going to bed. You'll just lie awake, probably feeling increasingly anxious about your inability to sleep – which will make it even harder to drop off.

Resist the urge to go to sleep too early. Even if you're dog tired at 9pm, don't head to bed just yet. If you do, you're likely to be wide awake in the early hours. Assuming you're getting up at around 7am, and provided you're feeling sleepy, it's best to go to bed at about 11pm or midnight.

Don't lie in bed awake: get up
It can be mystifying – and maddening. Although we're exhausted, although we've been looking forward all evening to being in

bed, when we finally get there we discover that we can't fall asleep.

If this happens to you, don't try to tough it out. If you're still awake 20 minutes after you've turned out the light, get up. Find somewhere quiet and not too brightly lit, and spend time doing something calming – reading a favourite book, perhaps, or meditating. When you feel sleepy, it's time to head back to bed. (You can use the same tactics if you wake up in the night and can't get back to sleep quickly.)

Don't let worry keep you awake

If you ask people when they worry most, they'll generally say first thing in the morning when they wake up and at night when they're lying in bed trying to sleep.

If worry is preventing you from getting a proper night's sleep, make sure you read Chapter 5. You'll find lots of really effective techniques for combating worry there. One you may find especially helpful at night is the idea of worry periods (see page 53).

A BRIEF WORD ABOUT SLEEPING TABLETS AND OTHER REMEDIES

Why not tackle insomnia by taking a sleeping tablet? They can certainly work in the short term and if you're really struggling to sleep your doctor may suggest them for a very limited period (zopiclone and temazepam are among those prescribed most often).

But they're not a long-term solution. You'll find that your body becomes used to the drug, meaning that you'll need to take larger doses to achieve the same results: clearly, that can't go on for ever. And it's not always straightforward to stop taking them – these sorts of drug can be quite addictive.

How about over-the-counter remedies like Nytol or Sleep-Eze? Again, these can be okay for a short while, but they're not herbal preparations: they tend to include an antihistamine. You may feel sleepy the following day. And just like sleeping tablets, your body will gradually become used to these remedies.

As for natural substances like valerian, chamomile and lavender, try them by all means. But there's little reliable scientific evidence at the moment to suggest that they really help.

The techniques we describe in this chapter have been proven to work. There are no side effects. You can use them for as long as you like and they won't lose their effectiveness. They're easy and they're free! And when you've tackled your sleep problems, you'll find that you feel less anxious. You'll be calmer, more optimistic, better able to cope with what life throws at you. But you probably know that already …

CHAPTER 12

How to eat (and drink) yourself to calmness

It's amazing how much of a difference we can make to our well-being just by getting the basics right.

Never underestimate the psychological power of eating properly, getting enough good-quality sleep and taking regular exercise. By looking after your body, you'll also be looking after your mind.

Take the results of a fascinating research project carried out in London recently. Over a two-year period, psychologists tracked the mental health of more than 10,000 people living in some of the most deprived areas of the city. Two findings stood out.

The first was that the individuals who increased their level of physical exercise felt happier – which is why we recommend exercise as a strategy to tackle anxiety.

The second finding was just as remarkable. The researchers discovered that simply improving diet – even without making any other lifestyle changes – was enough to cause a significant upswing in well-being. By eating and drinking better, the people in the London study felt less anxious and depressed, and calmer, more peaceful and more content.

We're all used to hearing that we can improve our physical health by changing our lifestyle. Well, it's just the same with our psychological well-being. By making some alterations to our daily routine we can make a real difference to our mood.

Those alterations don't need to be huge or complicated; even relatively small changes will help. We'll find it easier to appreciate and enjoy the good things in our life. And we'll be able to cope much better with the inevitable stresses and strains.

Elsewhere in this book you'll find information on how to build more physical exercise into your week (Chapter 9) and how to ensure you get the right amount of sleep (Chapter 11). So let's look now at the third strategy for healthy living: improving your diet. In a moment, we'll focus on what we should be eating and drinking. But we'll start with a few words on when we should be getting our nourishment.

A HEALTHY DIET FOR MIND AND BODY: THE WHEN

Doubtless you've already heard that 'breakfast is the most important meal of the day'. Maybe your parents mentioned it as you gulped down half a glass of juice or a mouthful of toast before hurrying off to school or work. Perhaps you've even been known to say something of the sort to your own children or partner.

Whether breakfast outranks lunch or dinner in importance is debatable. But there's no doubting the benefits of a nutritious breakfast.

Of course, many of us are skilled at finding reasons to skip our morning meal. We may be in such a rush that there doesn't seem to be time to eat. We may not feel particularly hungry early in the day. And those of us who are trying to lose weight may have convinced ourselves that breakfast is one meal we can easily do without.

Yet we have to remember that our body is designed to be refuelled at regular intervals. When our energy levels drop – and bear in mind that by the time you wake in the morning it will probably be around 12 hours since you've eaten – we need to replenish them. If we don't, we'll soon feel anxious, irritable or low.

In fact, hunger is so unpleasant that we're programmed to deal with it as soon as we can – which is why going without a bowl of muesli at 7.30am can lead to us filling up on biscuits, crisps, pastries and chocolate at 11am. Indeed, scientists have recently suggested that not eating when we get up makes high-calorie foods seem more attractive to our brain. The brain's intention is good: it wants to help us avoid starvation. But what tends to happen is that people who skip breakfast are more likely to put on weight rather than lose it.

So make breakfast a priority. Fill up on healthy cereals (check the sugar and salt contents on the pack), fruit, yoghurt and wholewheat toast. Not only will you find it easier to resist the unhealthy stuff later in the morning, you'll feel a whole lot more energetic, too.

The same principles hold for the rest of the day. Try to avoid filling up on unhealthy snacks and instead make sure you eat lunch and dinner, preferably at roughly the same times each day and not too far apart. If you have lunch at 1pm, you're probably going to need dinner by about 7pm. If you don't, hunger will make those unhealthy, high-calorie snacks seem irresistible.

Which is not to say that you shouldn't consume anything at all between meals. An occasional treat is fine, of course – in fact, for many of us it may seem essential! But generally aim to snack on, say, fresh or dried fruit or wholewheat crackers. If that doesn't sound terribly appealing, you can console yourself with the thought that you'll be helping both your mind and your body. And when you indulge in the odd cake or bar of chocolate, you'll be doing so with a clean conscience!

A HEALTHY DIET FOR MIND AND BODY: THE WHAT

Okay, we've decided that we're going to improve our diet. So what exactly should we be eating and drinking?

Well, food and drink can be a great comforter. As we saw in Chapter 11, a glass of milk or cup of herbal tea and a healthy snack can be a great way to wind down for sleep. But you may be surprised to discover that the nutritional guidelines are actually very straightforward. Certain 'superfoods' are sometimes touted as being particularly calming – shrimps, or kiwi, or lentils, for example. But the scientific evidence can be summarised in nine key messages:

- ★ Don't overdo the caffeine.
- ★ Base your meals around starchy foods.
- ★ Eat plenty of fruit and vegetables.
- ★ Eat more fish.
- ★ Limit your intake of saturated fat.
- ★ Eat less sugar.
- ★ Limit your salt consumption.

★ Drink lots of liquid.

★ Be careful about your alcohol intake.

All these changes are well within your grasp. With a little planning and perhaps just a bit of determination too, you can soon make substantial improvements to your diet. But don't rush it. Take it step by step. After all, you may well be changing habits that you've built up over several years. So aim for one positive alteration a week. That may strike you as too cautious. You may be itching to change everything around right now. But think how far you'll have come in just a couple of months.

> *Aim for one positive alteration a week.*

Don't overdo the caffeine

Hands up if you don't feel human until you've had your first cup of tea or coffee in the morning. Do you structure your day around your hot drinks – the mid-morning latte, the lunchtime Americano, the afternoon cuppa ? Are you, even now, sipping a coffee or wondering whether it's time you put the kettle on?

As you'll know, tea and coffee are pretty much a national obsession, with oceans of the stuff consumed every day. They power us through our days, giving us that burst of energy many of us rely upon. And they're often a kind of social glue, too, providing the perfect excuse to take time out with friends and colleagues.

The energising properties of tea and coffee derive from the fact that they are both rich in caffeine. And caffeine (as we saw in Chapter 11) is a stimulant. As such, it's a double-edged sword: it can revive and revitalise, but it can also make us feel jumpy, on edge – and anxious.

Caffeine can have this effect on anyone, regardless of their underlying emotional state. For people already struggling with anxiety, it can certainly make things worse. So if you're going through a difficult patch, cut down on your caffeine. Try herbal and fruit teas, or switch to decaffeinated coffee. And remember that caffeine is also present in many cola and so-called energy soft drinks.

Base your meals around starchy foods

Despite the publicity generated by certain carbohydrate-light diets, starchy carbs such as bread, rice, cereals, pasta and potatoes ought to make up around a third of our food intake. They're rich in key nutrients such as fibre, calcium, iron and B vitamins. They're also packed with energy: they provide us with the fuel we need to keep going until the next meal. Because we aren't hungry, we're much less likely to resort to relatively unhealthy snacks. There's no gap to fill!

So starchy foods should be an absolutely central part of our diet. If we really want to do it right, we should go for whole-wheat or wholegrain varieties. They tend to be lower in calories and higher in many nutrients than their white-grain cousins. Now, we recognise that brown rice or wholewheat pasta may not be everyone's idea of a tasty supper. But do give them a try: we think you may be pleasantly surprised. And if you're not overly keen, why not consider alternating – or mixing – the whole- and white-grain versions?

Eat plenty of fruit and vegetables

This one is unlikely to come as a surprise: over the past few years we've all become used to the idea that we ought to be consuming at least five portions of fruit and vegetables per day.

Though the jury may be out on whether fruit and veg can significantly cut our chances of developing cancer, there's little doubt about the wider health benefits. People who eat plenty of fruit and vegetables are likely to be slimmer and fitter, and may be less vulnerable to a range of illnesses, including, for example, cardiovascular problems. They may also feel a lot better, too – both physically and psychologically.

So it really is worth upping your fruit and vegetable intake to the recommended level. If that seems tricky, remember that your five a day doesn't have to be made up solely of fresh items: juice, tinned and dried fruit and veg all count.

You may well be wondering how much is a portion. For dried items it's about 30 grams; for fresh or tinned fruit and vegetables you'll need to eat 80 grams; for juice it's 150ml. But you probably don't have 24/7 access to a set of weighing scales and a measuring jug: in which case, how do you know when you've eaten a portion of broccoli or banana, artichoke or apple? For guidance, visit **www.nhs.uk** and search for '5 a day'.

Eat more fish

Every so often the media lets us know about another so-called 'superfood' – an item so amazingly good for us that it's portrayed rather like some magical elixir of life. We don't want to fall into that trap here. However, there's plenty of evidence that regular consumption of oily fish (and the omega 3 fatty acids they're crammed full of) really can help us avoid heart disease.

Oily fish include salmon, mackerel, trout, herring, fresh tuna, sardines, pilchards and eels. This is not to say that other types of fish aren't worth bothering with: they most definitely are. All fish contains lots of protein, minerals and vitamins, so we should aim to eat it at least twice a week, with one of those meals including an oily fish.

If you're pregnant, or think you might want to become pregnant in the future, make sure you don't eat more than two portions of oily fish per week. For everyone else, the recommended weekly maximum is four portions.

Limit your intake of saturated fat

Given that so many foods are marketed as 'fat free', it's easy to get the impression that fat is intrinsically bad for us. Actually, we all need some fat in our diet. But fat comes in two basic types – saturated and unsaturated – and it's the second of those that is the relatively healthy one.

Consuming too much saturated fat can increase our levels of cholesterol, making us more vulnerable to heart disease. Unsaturated fat, meanwhile, works to reduce the amount of cholesterol in our blood.

You'll find high levels of saturated fat in foods such as meat pies, sausages, cured meats, hard cheese, butter and lard, pastry, cakes and biscuits, cream, soured cream and crème fraîche. Unsaturated fat is plentiful in vegetable oils (including sunflower, rapeseed and olive oil), oily fish, avocados, nuts and seeds.

It's a good idea to get into the habit of checking the label on the food you buy. The fat content is usually listed, though it may be unclear what's saturated and what's unsaturated fat. If you're concerned about your weight, or if you suspect the item may contain saturated fat, it's best to go for the low-fat option: less than 3g of total fat per 100g. Where the saturated fat content is given, we should all limit our intake of high-fat (5g per 100g) and medium-fat items (1.5–5g per 100g). Low-fat is classed as anything containing less than 1.5g of saturated fat per 100g.

Eat less sugar

Most of us love sugary foods and they're fine as an occasional treat: the odd chocolate bar or cake can be a brilliant way of boosting our mood. But of course there's a downside. For one thing, that sugar rush doesn't last long, and when it wears off we can feel a bit low. And sugar is very high in junk calories: if we eat too much of it – as a large proportion of the population does – we quickly put on weight. Being overweight is not only risky for our physical health, it can also have a negative effect on our psychological well-being. Feeling fat is no fun. Our confidence and self-esteem can take a knock and our mood can nosedive.

Aim to limit your sugar intake – and remember that it's not just food that can be high in the stuff: many drinks, both alcoholic and non-alcoholic, are also full of sugar. As with fat, check the label: you may be surprised at just how much sugar there is in many items. Be especially wary of foods containing more than 5g of sugar per 100g.

Limit your salt consumption

Official UK guidelines recommend that adults consume no more than 6g of salt per day. This may not seem like great news for those of us who are partial to salty snacks. But the evidence is hard to ignore. By keeping our salt intake within safe limits, we'll reduce our risk of developing high blood pressure and of suffering the cardiovascular problems – such as strokes and heart attacks – that so often go with it.

Cut down on the salt you use when you cook. Try not to add it at the meal table. You'll be amazed at how quickly your taste buds will adjust.

Again, check the label on the food you buy: it's reckoned that around three-quarters of the salt we consume is contained in shop-bought items such as bread and breakfast cereals. In recent years many manufacturers have cut the salt content of their produce. Nevertheless, it may still be much higher than you might expect. High-salt foods are those that have more than 1.5g of salt (or 0.6g of sodium) per 100g. Low-salt items contain less than 0.3g of salt (or 0.1g of sodium) per 100g.

Drink lots of liquid

Many of us underestimate the importance of staying properly hydrated. Yet water makes up around two-thirds of the human body, and we use up that water every second of the day and night. If we don't drink enough, we soon feel the effects: headache, tiredness and an inability to concentrate are just three of the consequences we can personally vouch for.

To prevent yourself becoming dehydrated, aim to drink about 1.2 litres of liquid each day. Bear in mind that if the weather is hot, or you've been particularly active, you'll need to up your intake. Water is best, though milk, tea and fruit juice are good, too. Don't go for sugary drinks or alcohol though.

Be careful about your alcohol intake

Uh oh, you may be thinking, first they tell me to cut back on my beloved coffee; now they're going to advise me to stop drinking...

Not a bit of it. For many of us, a beer or a glass of wine with friends is one of life's real pleasures – a time when our problems, worries and fears are forgotten. If that's the case for you, we certainly wouldn't suggest you give it up, provided you're drinking within safe limits.

Experts recommend that men should regularly drink no more than 3–4 units a day; for women the limit is 2–3 units a day. A 175ml glass of wine contains around 2 units; a pint of ordinary-strength beer or cider contains roughly 2 units; and there are about 3 units in a pint of strong beer or cider. Alcopops usually contain around 1.5 units, while a small pub measure of spirits (25ml) equates to approximately 1 unit. If you've overdone it, you should steer clear of booze for at least 48 hours after-wards. Drinking more than this on a regular basis can put us at risk of health problems – both physical and psychological.

Of course, if we're feeling anxious or stressed or low, we might well be tempted to drink more than we would do normally. Alcohol can seem like a refuge or an escape. But any positive effects are strictly temporary. The next day, whatever has been bothering us won't have gone away – and we're now hungover and exhausted (as we saw in Chapter 11, alcohol can really mess up our sleep pattern). All in all, if we're drinking too much, our mood isn't going to improve – in fact, it's likely to head downhill.

So keep track of your alcohol intake. Stay within the recom-mended guidelines. If you're struggling with anxiety (or other emotional problems), try a few dry days – you may well be surprised at how much better you feel.

Sometimes when we're very stressed or anxious, it can seem as though only some dramatic change will make a difference

– that things will improve only if we somehow turn our life upside down. In fact, relatively small steps – such as modest improvements to our diet – can produce amazing effects. There's no need to go overboard: aim for a steady succession of small changes in what you eat and drink. And, as the weeks pass and the effects build, you'll feel your anxiety weaken and your mood lift.

CHAPTER 13

What is an anxiety disorder and how do I go about getting more help?

Everyone gets anxious – which is why we've written *How to Keep Calm and Carry On*. We want to set out the range of strategies and techniques you can use to overcome your anxiety and get on with the rest of your life.

Very probably, that will do the trick. But what if your anxiety is more deeply engrained? What if it won't shift? What if it's stopping you from functioning normally? What if you're suffering from what mental health professionals call an anxiety disorder? If you find yourself in this position, this book will still be very helpful. But you may also want to explore other sources of help.

ANXIETY DISORDERS

We'll talk through the options for additional help on page 154. But first let's pin down exactly what we mean by an anxiety disorder. There are six main types and in the following pages we give a brief introduction to each:

★ Phobias

★ Social phobia

★ Panic disorder

★ Generalised anxiety disorder

★ Obsessive-compulsive disorder

★ Post-traumatic stress disorder.

The term 'anxiety disorder' may be a bit frightening for some people. It can sound horribly medical – scarily 'psychiatric'. But it's worth bearing in mind that anxiety disorders are, with depression, by far the most common of all psychological problems. A wide-ranging survey of UK adults in 2007, for example, found that around one in ten people were suffering from anxiety and depression (the two often go together). The main US survey of mental health reported that almost one in five adults had experienced an anxiety disorder in the previous 12 months – equivalent to around 40 million people.

> *If you're struggling to cope with your anxiety, you are most definitely not alone.*

So if you're struggling to cope with your anxiety, you are most definitely not alone. In fact, although you may not realise it, you almost certainly know someone who has experienced an anxiety disorder at some point in their life. There is, as they say, a great deal of it about.

Phobias

People often use the word 'phobia' to describe the way they feel about something they dislike: *I'm a bit phobic about cats.*

I have a cheese phobia. I think he has a work phobia. But what does a psychologist mean when they use the term?

Well, a phobia is a really intense, exaggerated fear of something. And it's unrealistic: in truth, the person has little or nothing to be scared of. A phobia has a dramatic effect on the person's well-being: it may interfere with their relationships, their work, their ability to enjoy everyday life.

How does a person with a phobia feel when they encounter – or maybe even just think about – the object or situation they dread? Terrible. They panic. They might experience shortness of breath, sweating, chest pains, trembling, a choking feeling, dizziness, numbness, tingling in the limbs, nausea. They might also feel as though they're going to faint. (If this is something you've gone through, it's worth bearing in mind that you're not going to faint, no matter how much it seems like it. As we saw in Chapter 3, fainting occurs when our blood pressure plunges, and fear has exactly the opposite effect: it causes our blood pressure to sky-rocket. There is an exception though: blood-injection-injury phobias can indeed produce a drop in blood pressure.)

There are dozens and dozens of phobias. In fact, think of an object or situation and you can be reasonably certain that someone, somewhere is afraid of it.

Nevertheless, some phobias are far more common than others. Here are the top six, in descending order:

★ Animals
★ Heights
★ Blood
★ Enclosed spaces

★ Water

★ Flying.

Experts tend to classify phobias into five main groups:

★ *Animal phobias*, with some of the most commonly dreaded creatures being insects, dogs, snakes and rats.

★ *Natural environment phobias*, such as the fear of heights, water and storms.

★ *Situational phobias*, with the fears of flying and enclosed spaces leading the way but also including public transport, tunnels, bridges, lifts and driving.

★ *Blood-injection-injury phobias*, which include the fear of seeing blood, or of having an injection, or of suffering an injury.

★ *Everything else!* Among the most common of these other phobias are the fear of choking and of catching an illness.

There's nothing unusual about phobias, with perhaps around 10 per cent of people having experienced one in the last 12 months. If you have one phobia, there's a good chance that you'll have others, too.

The very good news, however, is that just one or two sessions with a trained therapist is often enough to help people overcome their phobia. Like the other anxiety disorders, there's absolutely no need to soldier on with phobias: solutions that really work are out there.

Social phobia

Many people feel nervous in social situations. Lots of us aren't keen on public speaking. And pretty much everyone has felt shy at some point in their lives.

Social phobia – or social anxiety disorder as it's sometimes called – is that everyday anxiety magnified many, many times over. People with the disorder always find social interaction incredibly difficult and distressing. They assume that they're terrible at it, while everyone else seems like a carefree social star. And they fear that these apparently calm and confident people will judge them as stupid or weak or incompetent.

Exactly which social situations produce this effect varies from individual to individual. Some find pretty much all social interaction extremely stressful. For others it's one particular situation: public speaking is a very common one, but social phobia can centre on a wide range of activities, including eating in company, dating, or even using a public toilet. Not surprisingly, people with social phobia will do everything they can to avoid the kinds of situations that will trigger their anxiety.

Experts have noticed that people with social phobia react to the situations they fear in a very distinct way. Instead of engaging with the people around them, their attention shifts inwards. *How am I performing? I'm making a complete mess of this. I don't know what to do or say. I feel terrible. It must be obvious that I can't cope.*

Images fill their mind. They 'see' themselves floundering; they visualise the anxiety etched on their face; they picture the bemusement on the faces of the people they're with. And of course the more they concentrate on these unhappy thoughts and images, the worse they feel.

Social phobia is very common. Some studies have suggested that around 13 per cent of us will experience it at some point in our life, with roughly 7 per cent of people suffering from it at any one time.

Panic disorder

You know that feeling when your computer has just swallowed a document you forgot to save? Or when you get to the airport and can't find your ticket? Or when you close the front door as you leave the house and then remember that your keys are still inside? We call that feeling panic: the sudden, unpleasant realisation that something bad might have happened. And it's no fun. But it's a walk in the park compared with what people with panic disorder typically experience.

True panic feels overwhelming – uncontrollable fear that makes it hard to breathe, that sets the heart pounding as if it were about to burst, that makes us tremble, or feel dizzy, or nauseous. It can seem as if we're about to collapse, or go crazy, or even die.

Panic attacks are a common feature of each of the anxiety disorders, but in panic disorder they take centre stage. For a start, the attacks tend to be more regular and frequent – and, initially at least, to occur out of the blue. The individual doesn't simply have to endure the horrible 10 or 20 minutes that an attack typically lasts; they spend a lot of time afterwards worrying about their panic. *Why did it happen? Is it a symptom of some serious physical or mental illness? When will it strike again?* One of the questions that weighs most heavily is: *what can I do to avoid another attack?*

Panic disorder changes the way people behave, most dramatically by causing them to steer clear of situations that they think might trigger a recurrence. If the first attack took place in a plane, for example, the person may decide not to fly again. If it happened in a lift, they'll take the stairs in future. And if it struck in the street, they may even begin to fear venturing out alone.

It's thought that about one in five people have experienced a panic attack at some point in their life, usually during a period of great stress. As for panic disorder, around 2 per cent of the population is affected at any one time.

Generalised anxiety disorder

We've spent quite a lot of this book discussing the effects of worry and outlining the techniques we can use to overcome it. The reason we've devoted so much space to it is that worry is such a big part of anxiety – and such a drain on our energy and enthusiasm.

In generalised anxiety disorder (GAD), worry runs riot. Imagine worrying for months on end, pretty much from the moment you wake up to the time you finally fall asleep, and with little or no reason. Imagine an existence in which your number-one priority is to avoid the catastrophe that you're somehow sure is just around the corner. Imagine worry so overwhelming and persistent that, no matter how careful you are, you never seem able to relax: instead, you're constantly on edge, irritable, exhausted. This is what it can feel like to live with GAD.

Around 3 per cent of people suffer from GAD. And like almost all anxiety problems, it seems to be much more common among women than men.

Obsessive-compulsive disorder

The names of some of the anxiety disorders may be unfamiliar (generalised anxiety disorder, for instance, doesn't seem to get a lot of exposure). But with obsessive-compulsive disorder (OCD) it's different. Thanks in part to celebrities such as Cameron Diaz, Jessica Alba and Paul Gascoigne talking openly about their struggles with the illness, OCD has well and truly entered the mainstream. Yet though we may know the name, and have a rough sense of what the disorder involves, when it comes to the details we may well be a little sketchy. So, what exactly is OCD?

At its heart are *obsessions*: upsetting thoughts, images and impulses that seem to be constantly intruding into the person's mind, sometimes throughout the day and night. Among the most common obsessions are:

★ fear of contamination from dirt or germs;

★ unwanted aggressive thoughts;

★ upsetting sexual fantasies;

★ blasphemous thoughts;

★ worries about breaking social rules (shouting in church, for instance);

★ doubts about whether a task has been completed satisfactorily (turning off the oven, writing an email without spelling mistakes, speaking to someone without offending them);

★ anxiety about what might happen if objects, words or numbers aren't arranged in a particular way;

★ fears about losing things.

What all these thoughts have in common is the idea of possible harm – emotional or social, physical or psychological. Because the idea of hurting oneself or other people is so distressing, individuals with OCD use a range of rituals in order to prevent that harm, or alternatively to stop the obsessions appearing in their mind. These rituals are called *compulsions*. They might be actions (cleaning, for example, or checking that the front door is locked) or thoughts (repeating a certain phrase, perhaps, or counting).

When things get really bad, these obsessions and compulsions can take over people's lives. OCD can become almost a full-time occupation. People who are afraid of contamination, for example, can spend literally hours each day washing themselves and cleaning the house. Leading a normal life becomes more or less impossible.

Around 2–3 per cent of us will develop OCD at some stage of our life. A major survey of adult Americans found that 1.2 per cent had suffered from OCD in the previous 12 months. Usually the obsessions and compulsions related to checking, hoarding and ordering. On average, obsessions took up a remarkable 5.9 hours a day, and compulsions 4.6 hours (with many people spending a lot longer than that). Given the astonishing amount of time OCD devours, you probably won't be surprised to learn that almost two-thirds of those who had experienced the illness in the previous year reported that it had severely disrupted their day-to-day life.

Post-traumatic stress disorder

When something awful happens to us, or to the people around us, it's natural to feel shaken up. We may find it tough to sleep, or to concentrate. We may find it impossible to stop thinking about what we've experienced. We'll probably feel upset, depressed, angry or guilty – and sometimes all of these and more.

For most of us, these feelings pass in time. We heal. But for some people, the wounds stay fresh. These individuals find themselves plagued by nightmares or flashbacks, when it feels as though they're experiencing the trauma all over again. They're always on edge, constantly alert for any reminder of what they've been through. No matter how hard they try to forget – sometimes by using alcohol or drugs – they can't shake off the distressing thoughts and memories.

When these problems persist for more than a month, the person may be suffering from post-traumatic stress disorder (PTSD). The 'trauma' is generally an event with the potential to cause death or serious injury – for example, major traffic accidents, potentially fatal illnesses, sexual assault, physical attack, violent robbery and mugging, the sudden death of a loved one, military combat, torture, or natural disasters. Some experts, though, think that the symptoms of PTSD are just as likely to be triggered by a broader range of problems, such as chronic illness, unemployment and divorce.

It's thought that around 5–10 per cent of people will experience PTSD during their lifetime. Some traumas seem to be more damaging than others. One US survey found that women were most likely to develop PTSD as a result of rape, sexual molestation, physical attack, being threatened with a weapon and childhood physical abuse. For men, the picture was different, with PTSD most commonly following rape, combat exposure, childhood neglect and childhood physical abuse.

GETTING MORE HELP

If you think you may be suffering from an anxiety disorder, it's time to get help. Chances are this book will make a really positive difference to how you feel. But you may also benefit from the personal assistance of a qualified professional.

We know those are words that, generally speaking, no one likes to hear. And it can be tough to take the first steps. People sometimes feel ashamed, apprehensive, embarrassed. But you can be absolutely sure that you're doing the right thing.

Start by having a chat with your family doctor. You'll probably find that just taking the plunge like this will raise your spirits. And your doctor will be able to talk through with you the options for treatment.

What works best? Well, a mass of research has shown that the most effective treatment for anxiety problems is psychological therapy, and particularly the type called *cognitive behaviour therapy* (CBT).

> *We may believe that we're in far more danger than is really the case.*

As we saw in the early chapters of this book, anxiety is what we feel when we believe we're in danger. It's a product of our thoughts, our interpretation of events. But if our thoughts are often negative, if we tend to misinterpret what's going on around us, we may believe that we're in far more danger than is really the case. And we'll feel unnecessarily anxious.

CBT will teach you to identify the negative thoughts fuelling anxiety – and to change them. (You'll probably have noticed that this sounds a lot like much of what we do in *How to Keep Calm and Carry On*. It's no coincidence. Our research and clinical work is very much CBT-based and so we draw heavily on CBT techniques in this book.)

CBT is mainly provided by clinical psychologists, though increasing numbers of psychiatrists, counsellors and nurses are being trained in this approach. In the UK, a concerted effort to make CBT more widely available has resulted in the Improving Access to Psychological Therapies scheme, which has trained 3,600 new therapists. Your doctor will be able to put you in touch with a CBT specialist. But if you're considering seeing a private therapist, make sure that they're properly qualified and that they've been specifically trained in CBT. The easiest way to do this is to check with an appropriate professional body, such as the British Association for Behavioural and Cognitive Psychotherapies.

Anxiety is also treated with medication, though which kind is used will depend on the individual's personal situation. For short-term help in a crisis, benzodiazepines are often prescribed. These can be very effective, but the body gets used to them pretty quickly, meaning that ever stronger doses are needed. And they can be addictive. For longer-term use, doctors will generally suggest one of the new breed of SSRI antidepressants. Again, many people find these drugs helpful. But, like all medicines, they can have side effects. Giving them up can be tricky, too.

All in all, medication can work. But the improvements brought about by CBT can often be greater, and typically last longer. That's why the UK's National Institute for Health and Clinical Excellence recommends CBT as the first line of treatment for each of the anxiety disorders.

When we're struggling with anxiety, it can seem as if there's no way out. We may believe that things will never improve; that there is nothing to be done; that we are somehow, and permanently, 'broken'.

But it isn't so. We are all far stronger, and more resilient, than we know. Moreover, treatment for anxiety disorders – and specifically psychological therapies – has made huge strides in recent years. Effective treatment truly is out there. If you're struggling to cope with your anxiety, make sure you seek it out.

FURTHER READING

If you'd like to read more about the issues covered in *How to Keep Calm and Carry On*, we've devoted a large section to anxiety in *Know Your Mind: Everyday Emotional and Psychological Problems and How to Overcome Them* (Rodale, 2009). You might also like to take a look at our book *Anxiety: A Very Short Introduction* (Oxford University Press, 2012). In *You Can Be Happy: The Scientifically Proven Way to Change How You Feel* (Pearson, 2012) we provide practical advice on how to overcome negative feelings and boost positive emotions.

We also recommend:

★ Gillian Butler, *Overcoming Social Anxiety and Shyness* (Robinson, 2009)

★ Melanie Fennell, *Overcoming Low Self-Esteem* (Robinson, 1999)

★ Ad Kerkhof, *Stop Worrying: Get Your Life Back on Track with CBT* (McGraw-Hill, 2010)

★ Warren Mansell, *Coping with Fears and Phobias* (Oneworld, 2007)

★ Kevin Meares and Mark Freeston, *Overcoming Worry* (Robinson, 2008)

★ Barbara Olasov Rothbaum, Edna Foa and Elizabeth Hembree, *Reclaiming Your Life from a Traumatic Experience* (Oxford University Press, 2007)

★ Derrick Silove and Vijaya Manicavasagar, *Overcoming Panic and Agoraphobia* (Robinson, 2009)

★ David Veale and Rob Willson, *Overcoming Obsessive-Compulsive Disorder* (Robinson, 2009)

★ Mark Williams and Danny Penman, *Mindfulness: A Practical Guide to Finding Peace in a Frantic World* (Piatkus, 2011)

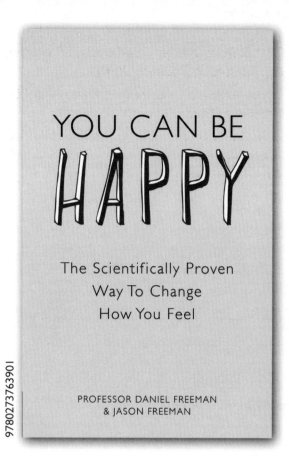

YOU CAN BE

HAPPY

The Scientifically Proven
Way To Change
How You Feel

9780273763901

PROFESSOR DANIEL FREEMAN
& JASON FREEMAN

Place happiness truly within your grasp
with this simple, practical guide to feeling
happier using the principles of CBT.

Nobody else can make you happy.
But you can. Here's all the help you need.

eBOOK
also available

The definitive guide to CBT – what it is, how it works, and how to use it in your life.

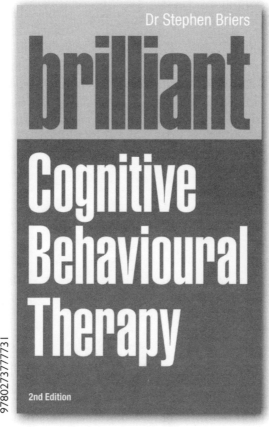